SPEAK UP, SPEAK OUT

Derek O'Brien was born in Kolkata. He studied at St Xavier's Collegiate School, Kolkata; St Columba's School, New Delhi; and Scottish Church College, Kolkata. During his school and college life he participated in numerous public speaking competitions, where he won multiple awards.

Derek began his professional career as a sports journalist but soon shifted to advertising. He worked for a number of years as creative head of Ogilvy. However, his natural ability in public speaking led Derek to focus all his energy and talent in his passion—quizzing.

Today, Derek O'Brien is Asia's best-known quizmaster and the CEO of Derek O'Brien & Associates Pvt. Ltd.

He has also written more than forty reference and quiz books, including two extremely successful school-textbook series: *Know and Grow with Derek* and *Be a GK Champ*.

He is at present a member of parliament, and also the chief whip of the Trinamool Congress, in the Rajya Sabha.

To know more about Derek O'Brien and his company, visit their website www.derek.in. You can also connect with him through Facebook and on Twitter, where his handle is @quizderek.

SPEAK UP, SPEAK OUT

MY FAVOURITE **ELOCUTION** PIECES
AND HOW TO DELIVER THEM

DEREK O'BRIEN

RED
TURTLE

Published in Red Turtle by
Rupa Publications India Pvt. Ltd. 2013
7/16, Ansari Road, Daryaganj
New Delhi 110002

Sales Centres:

Allahabad Bengaluru Chennai
Hyderabad Jaipur Kathmandu
Kolkata Mumbai

ISBN: 978-81-291-2115-8

10 9 8 7 6 5 4 3 2 1

Typeset in Minion Pro 11/14.5

Printed by Replika Press Pvt. Ltd., Haryana

To my Dad and my Ma

CONTENTS

INTRODUCTION

What was my favourite subject when I was in school?

History? No.

Physics? No.

Math? Certainly not!

Through all my school years, the elocution period was easily the one I loved the most, followed closely by English literature. I was often at the wrong end of the merit list when math and science marks were announced, but I would look forward with eager anticipation to the three elocution 'exams' we had every year. Those were three special days when I would enjoy the wholehearted applause and appreciation of my classmates and teachers. I don't want to sound immodest, but I rarely came second in this exam.

I learnt a lot during the elocution competitions. They gave me a great sense of confidence and, after participating in so many, I never suffered from stage fright in my life. In school, the 'stage' was a low, narrow, wooden platform in front of the green board in the classroom. We were each given three minutes to deliver our 'piece'. Through those three minutes, forty-four pairs of eyes stared unblinkingly at me, while my performance was marked by a teacher who knew exactly how good or bad I was in the other subjects. She sat at the back of the class and marked us on various parameters: choice of piece, diction, projection, poise, etc.

One hopes that elocution (sometimes referred to as 'recitation' in primary classes) continues to be an integral part of school life, even though it is not a formal subject in the CBSE, ICSE and State Board curricula. A lot of what I do professionally today was learnt when I participated in those class elocution tests and at inter-school elocution contests.

Over the years, I have regularly received pleas for help. My friends have called: 'Hey, Nikhil needs a good piece for his elocution competition. What do you recommend?' or sent SMSs like: 'No poems allowed, can you suggest a good prose piece for Pooja's elocution? Pleeease!'

After answering these frantic queries for years, I thought, why not compile a book of my favourite elocution pieces? This book comprises all the poems that I have 'elocuted' in school, those said by others that I have liked, and some classic pieces that I have come across over the years. I would like to thank all my friends and their children, who inspired me to put this book together. If you folks had not called, *Speak Up, Speak Out* would never have been compiled.

So, if you are looking for a good piece, pick one from here that suits your style. You can read my introduction to each piece and my suggestions on how to speak it while making your selection. If you are the serious type, choose a serious piece; if you think you can handle a funny piece, there are quite a few of those too. My one advice is: be yourself. Don't try to be someone you are not.

Even if you are not taking part in an elocution test the day after tomorrow, go ahead and read the book. It is a collection of some of the best pieces of writing that I have known and enjoyed over the years.

Happy reading, and happy speaking.

With every good wish,

Derek O'Brien

WHAT IS ELOCUTION?

Speaking on stage is very much like learning to ride a bicycle. The first few times you think that it is absolutely impossible and that you will never succeed. Then suddenly, one day, you are able to pedal away and balance yourself without much help, and very soon you are confident enough to race with your friends.

The same goes with speaking in public. The only solution to stage fright is practice, practice, and more practice. Take every opportunity you get to air your views—be it saying something in class or to a group of friends.

The first step to being a good extempore speaker, a good actor or a good debater, is doing elocution. Elocution is the art of speaking correctly. It centres around a language, and its pronunciation, grammar and delivery. This includes articulation, inflection (modulation and pitch of the voice), accent (comparative stress on different syllables) and clarity of voice.

Elocution and acting on stage are different. An actor, apart from 'elocuting' the lines, depends heavily on body language—in the form of gestures and movement on stage—among other things. The elocutionist uses only his or her voice. Yes, the occasional hand movement is necessary to drive home a point, but excessive use of hands and moving around are a definite no-no.

In most elocution contests, participants memorize and deliver poems, prose pieces or famous speeches. Another form of elocution is the extempore. In this, the participants are given a common topic or different topics on which they have to speak. The topics can range from environmental issues like global warming, to social issues like corruption. The one major difference between the two is that in elocution you prepare and memorize the piece beforehand, whereas in extempore you are given around an hour to prepare.

Whatever the type of competition, contestants are usually given a time limit of five to six minutes. They are generally judged on: Choice of piece, Memory, Diction, Expression, Posture and Overall presentation.

Choice of piece: In some contests you are asked to choose your own piece. If you have the freedom to do so, make sure you choose one that suits you and which you are comfortable with.

Memory: It goes without saying that you should not forget your piece when you are halfway into speaking it! Make sure that you have memorized the piece thoroughly before concentrating on your expressions.

Diction: Your words need to be clear. Your audience must be able to understand what you are saying. Be extra careful that you do not trail off at the end of sentences or swallow your words.

Expression: You need to modulate your voice, sometimes you will need to be soft and sometimes a little louder. You must convey the feeling and emotion of your piece through your voice.

Posture: Be still while 'elocuting'. Don't sway from side to side, or make too many gestures. Stand comfortably, legs slightly apart, with your back straight. Be careful that you do not come across as too stiff either. Keep your hands loosely by your side, fingers curled into a gentle fist.

Overall presentation: It is extremely important that you choose a piece that suits you. If it does suit you, and your expression and diction are good, you should do well.

HOW TO CHOOSE AN ELOCUTION PIECE

To do well in an elocution contest, it is important that you choose

§   A good piece, and more importantly,
§   A piece that suits you.

If you are a big, strapping boy in Class IX or X, 'The Tiger and the Zebra' is not the piece for you. A prose piece like 'I Demand Death' would suit you fine, or definitely one of the speeches in this book.

Use your type of voice to your advantage. If you have a thin or high-pitched voice, go for a short story like 'The Emperor's New Clothes'.

So, choosing the correct piece for yourself is half the battle won. Get comfortable with it by understanding what it is trying to convey. If you have a problem with memorizing, select a rhyming piece—those are easier to learn. If you are good with facial expressions try out one of the funny pieces or even a powerful piece like 'The Son of Man'.

I have attempted to segregate the elocution pieces in this book under four heads: Junior School (classes VI and below), Middle School (classes VI-VIII), Middle to Senior School and Senior School (classes IX and upwards). This is just a guide; if you would prefer to choose a piece from a different grade, go ahead. Just make sure that you are comfortable saying it.

HOW TO PREPARE YOUR ELOCUTION PIECE

§ Once you have chosen the piece, read it a couple of times. Understand what the poet or author is saying. More important, understand what is not said; understand the situation.

§ Ensure that the poem is of the required length, depending on the time allotted to you.

§ Next, you need to get down to memorizing it. Go in for expressions only after you have memorized the piece properly.

§ Take a pencil and underline the words and sentences you need to stress on. Circle the words you need to speak softly.

§ Practise aloud! Make sure that every word is audible and clear. Many of us tend to swallow the ends of sentences. Your voice should be clear and distinct. Try this little trick that I follow: first say your piece very slowly, moving like a goods train, with no expression, enunciating every word and syllable. Next, rattle off the piece like an express train. Alternate a few times between fast and slow. This will also help you memorize the piece better.

§ Don't speak too fast. Many of us, when nervous, tend to rush through the piece. Be relaxed! Take your time.

§ Make sure that you are not reciting in a sing-song manner. We did that when we recited nursery rhymes in kindergarten, but that's not how we do elocution. Bring your voice down at the end of sentences and be sure not to take off like a jet plane as you begin the next sentence.

§ Don't suddenly develop a foreign accent. Speak in your own voice. If you are doing Barack Obama's 'Yes We Can Change' speech, please don't use an American accent and try to sound like him. Remember, you are not being judged on how similar you sound to the original speaker. Similarly, if you are doing 'Why Can't the English' from *My Fair Lady*, please don't half sing it like Henry Higgins did in the film. He needed to, because the film was a musical; you are at an elocution contest, not *Indian Idol*.

§ Practise in front of a mirror. Remember, you are your best critic. Watch your facial expressions. Make sure they are in sync with what you are saying.

§ Now, start concentrating on the two Es: Expression and Enunciation. Feel the piece. If you are reciting Hans Christian Andersen's 'The Emperor's New Clothes', become the storyteller—captivate your audience, modulate your voice. For example, in this piece, you would need four distinct voices: the storyteller's, the emperor's, the weavers' and the officials'. Don't speak in the same tone throughout the story. Make it interesting…make it exciting. Your speech should resemble a moving train—sometimes you need to go slow, and sometimes you need to pick up speed. To stress on a particular point, you could drop your voice to a whisper, or be forceful.

§ Please don't use too many hand gestures and never walk around. As I said before, that is acting. In elocution, you are judged only on how you speak.

§ Watch your stance. How you stand is extremely important. The most common and comfortable posture is with your feet slightly apart, one a little in front of the other. Make sure that you are well balanced and relaxed. Keep your shoulders, back and spine upright and hands loosely at your sides. Don't clench your fists tight. Some prefer keeping their hands behind their backs. That's fine but be careful not to appear too stiff. Another disadvantage of clasping your hands behind your back is that when you want to make a small hand gesture, it would look unnatural bringing your hand to the front from behind.

§ Practise making eye contact. Remember to look at your audience—not at the ceiling or at your feet. If you are uncomfortable looking directly at someone, use the simple trick that many public speakers use. Choose five spots: front row left, front row right, centre hall left, centre hall right and centre hall middle. If you look at these five different spots while you speak, it will seem as if you are looking at everyone.

§ Now you are ready to go on stage! Before you go up, take a couple of deep breaths, loosen your body, and once your name is announced, walk smartly on to the stage. Be relaxed... Don't march! Once you reach your spot, take your position, look towards the audience for a few seconds and then begin. When you have finished, don't walk off abruptly. Remain there for a few seconds and then smartly walk back to your seat.

POETRY

A LEGEND OF THE NORTHLAND

Phoebe Cary

This piece is written in simple rhyme, making it easy to memorize. There is not much scope in this for variation in voice, but it is a good piece to show how well you can enunciate (pronounce the words).

Away, away in the Northland,
Where the hours of the day are few,
And the nights are so long in winter,
They cannot sleep them through;

Where they harness the swift reindeer
To the sledges, when it snows;
And the children look like bears' cubs
In their funny, furry clothes:

They tell them a curious story—
I don't believe 'tis true;
And yet you may learn a lesson
If I tell the tale to you.

Once, when the good Saint Peter
Lived in the world below,
And walked about it, preaching,
Just as he did, you know;

He came to the door of a cottage,
In travelling round the earth,
Where a little woman was making cakes,
And baking them on the hearth;

And being faint with fasting,
For the day was almost done,
He asked her, from her store of cakes,
To give him a single one.

So she made a very little cake,
But as it baking lay,
She looked at it, and thought it seemed
Too large to give away.

Therefore she kneaded another,
And still a smaller one;
But it looked, when she turned it over,
As large as the first had done.

Then she took a tiny scrap of dough,
And rolled, and rolled it flat;
And baked it thin as a wafer—
But she couldn't part with that.

For she said, 'My cakes that seem too small
When I eat of them myself,
Are yet too large to give away.'
So she put them on the shelf.

Then good Saint Peter grew angry,
For he was hungry and faint;
And surely such a woman
Was enough to provoke a saint.

And he said, 'You are far too selfish
To dwell in a human form,
To have both food and shelter,
And fire to keep you warm.'

'Now, you shall build as the birds do,
And shall get your scanty food
By boring, and boring, and boring,
All day in the hard dry wood.'

Then up she went through the chimney,
Never speaking a word,
And out of the top flew a woodpecker.
For she was changed to a bird.

She had a scarlet cap on her head,
And that was left the same,
But all the rest of her clothes were burned
Black as a coal in the flame.

And every country school boy
Has seen her in the wood;
Where she lives in the woods till this very day,
Boring and boring for food.

And this is the lesson she teaches:
Live not for yourself alone,
Lest the needs you will not pity
Shall one day be your own.

Give plenty of what is given to you,
Listen to pity's call;
Don't think the little you give is great,
And the much you get is small.

Now, my little boy, remember that,
And try to be kind and good,
When you see the woodpecker's sooty dress,
And see her scarlet hood.

You mayn't be changed to a bird, though you live
As selfishly as you can;
But you will be changed to a smaller thing—
A mean and selfish man.

THE JUMBLIES
Edward Lear

Edward Lear is the master of nonsense verse, a form of whimsical and humorous poetry depicting peculiar characters in amusing and fantastical situations. He often uses fanciful phrases and meaningless made-up words. This piece displays various emotions which are expressed by the use of a variety of metaphors, similes and onomatopoeia. It is ideal for someone in junior school taking part in an elocution contest for the first time.

I
They went to sea in a Sieve, they did,
    In a Sieve they went to sea:
In spite of all their friends could say,
On a winter's morn, on a stormy day,
    In a Sieve they went to sea!
And when the Sieve turned round and round,
And every one cried, 'You'll all be drowned!'
They called aloud, 'Our Sieve ain't big,
But we don't care a button! we don't care a fig!
    In a Sieve we'll go to sea!'
            Far and few, far and few,
                Are the lands where the Jumblies live;
            Their heads are green, and their hands are blue,
                And they went to sea in a Sieve.

II

They sailed away in a Sieve, they did,
    In a Sieve they sailed so fast,
With only a beautiful pea-green veil
Tied with a riband by way of a sail,
    To a small tobacco-pipe mast;
And every one said, who saw them go,
'O won't they be soon upset, you know!
For the sky is dark, and the voyage is long,
And happen what may, it's extremely wrong
    In a Sieve to sail so fast!'
      Far and few, far and few,
        Are the lands where the Jumblies live;
        Their heads are green, and their hands are blue,
        And they went to sea in a Sieve.

III

The water it soon came in, it did,
    The water it soon came in;
So to keep them dry, they wrapped their feet
In a pinky paper all folded neat,
    And they fastened it down with a pin.
And they passed the night in a crockery-jar,
And each of them said, 'How wise we are!
Though the sky be dark, and the voyage be long,
Yet we never can think we were rash or wrong,
    While round in our Sieve we spin!'
      Far and few, far and few,
        Are the lands where the Jumblies live;
        Their heads are green, and their hands are blue,
        And they went to sea in a Sieve.

IV

And all night long they sailed away;
   And when the sun went down,
They whistled and warbled a moony song
To the echoing sound of a coppery gong,
   In the shade of the mountains brown.
'O Timballo! How happy we are,
When we live in a Sieve and a crockery-jar,
And all night long in the moonlight pale,
We sail away with a pea-green sail,
   In the shade of the mountains brown!'
      Far and few, far and few,
         Are the lands where the Jumblies live;
         Their heads are green, and their hands are blue,
            And they went to sea in a Sieve.

V

They sailed to the Western Sea, they did,
   To a land all covered with trees,
And they bought an Owl, and a useful Cart,
And a pound of Rice, and a Cranberry Tart,
   And a hive of silvery Bees.
And they bought a Pig, and some green Jack-daws,
And a lovely Monkey with lollipop paws,
And forty bottles of Ring-Bo-Ree,
   And no end of Stilton Cheese.
      Far and few, far and few,
         Are the lands where the Jumblies live;
         Their heads are green, and their hands are blue,
            And they went to sea in a Sieve.

VI

And in twenty years they all came back,
  In twenty years or more,
And every one said, 'How tall they've grown!
For they've been to the Lakes, and the Torrible Zone,
  And the hills of the Chankly Bore!'
And they drank their health, and gave them a feast
Of dumplings made of beautiful yeast;
And every one said, 'If we only live,
We too will go to sea in a Sieve,—
  To the hills of the Chankly Bore!'
    Far and few, far and few,
      Are the lands where the Jumblies live;
      Their heads are green, and their hands are blue,
        And they went to sea in a Sieve.

THE NEW DUCKLING

Alfred Noyes

The poem tells us to just be ourselves, not someone we believe we should be, or who others think we should be! It teaches us to be satisfied with the way we are and not strive to be someone we cannot. It has lots of scope for expression and voice modulation, and is a winning piece.

'I want to be new,' said the duckling.
  'Oho!' said the wise old owl,
While the guinea hen cluttered off chuckling
  To tell all the rest of the fowl.

'I should like a more elegant figure,'

That child of a duck went on.
'I should like to grow bigger and bigger,
    Until I could swallow a swan.

'I *won't* be the bond slave of habit,
    I *won't* have these webs on my toes.
I want to run around like a rabbit
    A rabbit as red as a rose.'

'I *don't* want to waddle like mother,
    Or quack like my silly old dad.
I want to be utterly other,
    And *frightfully* modern and mad.'

'Do you know,' said the turkey, 'you're quacking!
    There's a fox creeping up thro' the rye;
And if you're not utterly lacking,
    You'll make for that duck pond. Good-bye!'

But the duckling was perky as perky,
    'Take care of your stuffing!' he called.
(This was horribly rude to a turkey!)
    'But you aren't a real turkey,' he bawled.

'You're an early-Victorian sparrow!
    A fox is more fun than a sheep!
I shall show that *my* mind is not narrow
    And give him my feathers to keep.'

Now the curious end of this fable,
    So far as the rest ascertained,
Though they searched from the barn to the stable,
    Was that *only his feathers remained.*

So he *wasn't* a bond slave of habit,
	And he *didn't* have webs on his toes;
And *perhaps* he runs round like a rabbit,
	A rabbit as red as a rose.

THE TIGER AND THE ZEBRA
Kenn Nesbitt

Kenn Nesbitt is an American children's poet who lives in Spokane, Washington. His poems are humorous and extremely popular around the world. In this hilarious piece the speaker has to recite in two voices—one of the sly tiger, the other of the easy-to-fool zebra. Have fun!

The tiger phoned the zebra
And invited him to dine.
He said 'If you could join me
That would simply be divine.'
The zebra said 'I thank you,
But respectfully decline.
I heard you ate the antelope;
He was a friend of mine.'

On hearing this the tiger cried
'I must admit it's true!
I also ate the buffalo,
the llama and the gnu.
And yes I ate the warthog,
The gazelle and kangaroo,
But I could never eat a creature
Beautiful as you.'

'You see I have a secret
I'm embarrassed to confide:
I look on you with envy
and a modicum of pride.
Of all the creatures ever known,'
The tiger gently sighed,
'It seems we are the only two
With such a stripy hide.

'Now seeing how we share this
Strong resemblance of the skin,
I only can conclude that we are
Just as close as kin.
This means you are my brother
And, though fearsome I have been,
I could not eat my brother,
That would surely be a sin.'

The zebra thought, and then replied
'I'm certain you are right.
The stripy coats we both possess
Are such a handsome sight!
My brother, will you let me
Reconsider if I might?
My calendar is empty so
Please let us dine tonight.'

The tiger met the zebra in
His brand-new fancy car
And drove him to a restaurant
Which wasn't very far.
And when they both were seated

At a table near the bar,
The zebra asked 'What's on the grill?'
The tiger said 'You are.'

'But please, you cannot dine on me!'
The outraged zebra cried.
'To cook me up and eat me
is a thing I can't abide.
You asked me for your trust
And I unwarily complied.
You said you could not eat me
Now you plan to have me fried?'

'And what about the envy
And the modicum of pride?
And what of us as brothers
Since we share a stripy hide?'
'I'm sorry,' said the tiger
And he smiled as he replied,
'But I love the taste of zebra
So, in other words, I lied.'

THE WALRUS AND THE CARPENTER

Lewis Carroll

This poem is from **Through the Looking Glass,** *recited by Tweedledum
and Tweedledee to Alice in chapter four. It is written in the style of a traditional
English ballad and is unique in its silliness. An extremely popular piece, it has been
recited in many classrooms across the country. If you choose to recite it, remember
to keep your voice and tone light—remember it is a funny piece.*

The sun was shining on the sea,
　　Shining with all his might:
He did his very best to make
　　The billows smooth and bright—
And this was odd, because it was
　　The middle of the night.

The moon was shining sulkily,
　　Because she thought the sun
Had got no business to be there
　　After the day was done—
'It's very rude of him,' she said,
　　'To come and spoil the fun!'

The sea was wet as wet could be,
　　The sands were dry as dry.
You could not see a cloud, because
　　No cloud was in the sky:
No birds were flying overhead—
　　There were no birds to fly.

The Walrus and the Carpenter
　　Were walking close at hand;
They wept like anything to see
　　Such quantities of sand:
'If this were only cleared away,'
　　They said, 'it would be grand!'

'If seven maids with seven mops
　　Swept it for half a year.
Do you suppose,' the Walrus said,
　　'That they could get it clear?'
'I doubt it,' said the Carpenter,
　　And shed a bitter tear.

'O Oysters, come and walk with us!'
    The Walrus did beseech.
'A pleasant walk, a pleasant talk,
    Along the briny beach:
We cannot do with more than four,
    To give a hand to each.'

The eldest Oyster looked at him,
    But never a word he said:
The eldest Oyster winked his eye,
    And shook his heavy head—
Meaning to say he did not choose
    To leave the oyster-bed.

But four young Oysters hurried up,
    All eager for the treat:
Their coats were brushed, their faces washed,
    Their shoes were clean and neat—
And this was odd, because, you know,
    They hadn't any feet.

Four other Oysters followed them,
    And yet another four;
And thick and fast they came at last,
    And more, and more, and more—
All hopping through the frothy waves,
    And scrambling to the shore.

The Walrus and the Carpenter
    Walked on a mile or so,
And then they rested on a rock
    Conveniently low:

And all the little Oysters stood
    And waited in a row.

'The time has come,' the Walrus said,
    'To talk of many things:
Of shoes—and ships—and sealing-wax—
    Of cabbages—and kings—
And why the sea is boiling hot—
    And whether pigs have wings.'

'But wait a bit,' the Oysters cried,
    'Before we have our chat;
For some of us are out of breath,
    And all of us are fat!'
'No hurry!' said the Carpenter.
    They thanked him much for that.

'A loaf of bread,' the Walrus said,
    'Is what we chiefly need:
Pepper and vinegar besides
    Are very good indeed—
Now if you're ready, Oysters dear,
    We can begin to feed.'

'But not on us!' the Oysters cried,
    Turning a little blue.
'After such kindness, that would be
    a dismal thing to do!'
'The night is fine,' the Walrus said.
    'Do you admire the view?

'It was so kind of you to come!
    And you are very nice!'
The Carpenter said nothing but

'Cut us another slice:
I wish you were not quite so deaf—
    I've had to ask you twice!'

'It seems a shame,' the Walrus said,
    'To play them such a trick,
After we've brought them out so far,
    And made them trot so quick!'
The Carpenter said nothing but
    'The butter's spread too thick!'

'I weep for you,' the Walrus said:
    'I deeply sympathize.'
With sobs and tears he sorted out
    Those of the largest size,
Holding his pocket-handkerchief
    Before his streaming eyes.

'O Oysters,' said the Carpenter,
    'You've had a pleasant run!
Shall we be trotting home again?'
    But answer came there none—
And this was scarcely odd, because
    They'd eaten every one.

WHAT IF DR SEUSS WROTE TECHNICAL MANUALS?
Gene Ziegler

Gene Ziegler is a semi-retired educator and information technology specialist. This poem became very popular on the Internet, and was often quoted without giving the poet credit. The original title is 'A Grandchild's Guide to Using Grandpa's

If a packet hits a pocket on a socket on a port,
And the bus is interrupted as a very last resort,
And the address of the memory makes your floppy disk
    abort,
Then the socket packet pocket has an error to report!

If your cursor finds a menu item followed by a dash,
And the double-clicking icons put your window in the
    trash,
And your data is corrupted 'cause the index doesn't hash,
Then your situation's hopeless, and your system's gonna
    crash!

If the label on your cable on the gable at your house,
Says the network is connected to the button on your
    mouse,
But your packets want to tunnel to another protocol,
That's repeatedly rejected by the printer down the hall.

And your screen is all distorted by the side effects of
    gauss,
So your icons in the window are as wavy as a souse,
Then you may as well reboot and go out with a bang,
'Cause as sure as I'm a poet, the sucker's gonna hang!

When the copy of your floppy's getting sloppy on the disk,
And the microcode instructions cause unnecessary RISC,
Then you have to flash your memory and you'll want to
    RAM your ROM,

Quickly turn off your computer and be sure to tell your
    mom!

TIGER
Keki N. Daruwalla

*A former IPS officer, who retired as additional director in the Research and
Analysis Wing (RAW), Keki Daruwalla received the Sahitya Akademi Award in
1984 for his poetry. This poem, which is a take-off on William Blake's immortal
poem 'Tyger', talks about the plight of our national animal and its endangerment.*

The tiger isn't burning bright
Either in shadow or in sun.
The tiger family is thinning
Two by two and one by one.

The tiger isn't burning bright.
In the forests of the night
Or in the wilderness of day.
We need to understand his plight.

The father Sheru's missing now.
Sheru has been shot and skinned
Poachers ground his bones to powder
For some Chinese medicine.

Bones would bring them power, they thought.
Put life into some sickly man.
Their souls were sick, killing tigers
Is something we won't understand.

His skin is hanging on the wall;

His bones are packed in plastic white
And shipped out. A gecko on the wall
Is hunting insects on his hide.

Once jungles trembled at his roar;
Tree tops flew up—birds disappeared!
Monkeys screamed (what an uproar!),
Now geckoes nibble on his ear!

Lord God had stamped upon his skin
In equal stripes both night and dawn.
His black-and-gold won't shimmer now.
Boar-hunter, Forest King—he's gone.

A VISIT FROM ST NICHOLAS

Clement Clarke Moore

This is a wonderful, easy-rhyming poem. It is also a good piece to say at a winter social gathering. There is enough scope to modulate your voice and use expressions here. Remember, it is a happy poem, so make sure your audience enjoys it as much as you.

'Twas the night before Christmas, when all through the
     house
Not a creature was stirring, not even a mouse;
The stockings were hung by the chimney with care,
In hopes that St Nicholas soon would be there;
The children were nestled all snug in their beds,
While visions of sugar-plums danced in their heads;
And mamma in her 'kerchief, and I in my cap,
Had just settled our brains for a long winter's nap,
When out on the lawn there arose such a clatter,
I sprang from the bed to see what was the matter.
Away to the window I flew like a flash,
Tore open the shutters and threw up the sash.
The moon on the breast of the new-fallen snow
Gave the lustre of mid-day to objects below,
When, what to my wondering eyes should appear,
But a miniature sleigh, and eight tiny reindeer,
With a little old driver, so lively and quick,
I knew in a moment it must be St Nick.
More rapid than eagles his coursers they came,
And he whistled, and shouted, and called them by name;
'Now, Dasher! Now, Dancer! Now, Prancer and Vixen!
On, Comet! On, Cupid! On, Donder and Blitzen!

To the top of the porch! To the top of the wall!
Now dash away! Dash away! Dash away all!'
As dry leaves that before the wild hurricane fly,
When they meet with an obstacle, mount to the sky;
So up to the house-top the coursers they flew,
With the sleigh full of toys, and St Nicholas too.
And then, in a twinkling, I heard on the roof
The prancing and pawing of each little hoof.
As I drew in my head, and was turning around,
Down the chimney St Nicholas came with a bound.
He was dressed all in fur, from his head to his foot,
And his clothes were all tarnished with ashes and soot;
A bundle of toys he had flung on his back,
And he looked like a peddler just opening his pack.
His eyes—how they twinkled! His dimples how merry!
His cheeks were like roses, his nose like a cherry!
His droll little mouth was drawn up like a bow
And the beard of his chin was as white as the snow;
The stump of a pipe he held tight in his teeth,
And the smoke it encircled his head like a wreath;
He had a broad face and a little round belly,
That shook when he laughed, like a bowlful of jelly.
He was chubby and plump, a right jolly old elf,
And I laughed when I saw him, in spite of myself;
A wink of his eye and a twist of his head,
Soon gave me to know I had nothing to dread;
He spoke not a word, but went straight to his work,
And filled all the stockings; then turned with a jerk,
And laying his finger aside of his nose,
And giving a nod, up the chimney he rose;
He sprang to his sleigh, to his team gave a whistle,

And away they all flew like the down of a thistle,
But I heard him exclaim, ere he drove out of sight,
'Happy Christmas to all, and to all a good-night.'

CASEY AT THE BAT

Ernest Lawrence Thayer

This is the story of a baseball game which ends in disaster. It has all the features one looks for in a good, narrative poem—a gripping story, a strong rhythm and a rhyme scheme that flows easily. This poem needs to be said with a lot of passion. Imagine yourself as a cricket commentator on radio, taking the viewers through the last over of a pulsating Twenty20 match. That's the excitement that you need to generate.

The outlook wasn't brilliant for the Mudville nine that day;
The score stood four to two, with but one inning more to
    play,
And then when Cooney died at first, and Barrows did the
    same,
A pall-like silence fell upon the patrons of the game.

A straggling few got up to go in deep despair. The rest
Clung to that hope which springs eternal in the human
    breast;
They thought, 'If only Casey could but get a whack at
    that—
We'd put up money even now, with Casey at the bat.'

But Flynn preceded Casey, as did also Jimmy Blake,
And the former was a hoodoo, while the latter was a cake;
So upon that stricken multitude grim melancholy sat,

For there seemed but little chance of Casey getting to the
     bat.

But Flynn let drive a single, to the wonderment of all,
And Blake, the much despisèd, tore the cover off the ball;
And when the dust had lifted, and men saw what had
     occurred,
There was Jimmy safe at second and Flynn a-hugging third.

Then from five thousand throats and more there rose a
     lusty yell;
It rumbled through the valley, it rattled in the dell;
It pounded on the mountain and recoiled upon the flat,
For Casey, mighty Casey, was advancing to the bat.

There was ease in Casey's manner as he stepped into his
     place;
There was pride in Casey's bearing and a smile lit Casey's
     face.
And when, responding to the cheers, he lightly doffed his
     hat,
No stranger in the crowd could doubt 'twas Casey at the
     bat.

Ten thousand eyes were on him as he rubbed his hands
     with dirt;
Five thousand tongues applauded when he wiped them on
     his shirt;
Then while the writhing pitcher ground the ball into his
     hip,
Defiance flashed in Casey's eye, a sneer curled Casey's lip.

And now the leather-covered sphere came hurtling through
     the air,

And Casey stood a-watching it in haughty grandeur there.
Close by the sturdy batsman the ball unheeded sped—
'That ain't my style,' said Casey. 'Strike one!' the umpire said.

From the benches, black with people, there went up a
    muffled roar,
Like the beating of the storm-waves on a stern and distant
    shore;
'Kill him! Kill the umpire!' shouted someone on the stand;
And it's likely they'd have killed him had not Casey raised
    his hand.

With a smile of Christian charity great Casey's visage shone;
He stilled the rising tumult; he bade the game go on;
He signalled to the pitcher, and once more the dun sphere
    flew;
But Casey still ignored it, and the umpire said, 'Strike two!'

'Fraud!' cried the maddened thousands, and echo answered
    'Fraud!'
But one scornful look from Casey and the audience was
    awed.
They saw his face grow stern and cold, they saw his
    muscles strain,
And they knew that Casey wouldn't let that ball go by
    again.

The sneer has fled from Casey's lip, his teeth are clenched
    in hate;
He pounds with cruel violence his bat upon the plate.
And now the pitcher holds the ball, and now he lets it go.
And now the air is shattered by the force of Casey's blow.

Oh, somewhere in this favoured land the sun is shining
    bright;
The band is playing somewhere, and somewhere hearts are
    light,
And somewhere men are laughing, and little children shout;
But there is no joy in Mudville—great Casey has struck out.

GUILTY OR NOT GUILTY

Anonymous

*I first heard this anonymous poem at an inter-school competition, being recited
by a twelve-year-old. It is a touching tale, and if your voice can reflect the deep
emotions expressed in this piece, it is a sure winner.*

She stood at the bar of justice,
    A creature wan and wild,
In form too small for a woman,
    In features too old for a child.
For a look so worn and pathetic
    Was stamped on her pale young face,
It seemed long years of suffering
    Must have left that silent trace.

'Your name?' said the judge, as he eyed her
    With kindly look yet keen,
'Is—?' 'Mary McGuire, if you please, sir.'
    'And your age?'—'I am turned fifteen.'
'Well, Mary—' and then from a paper
    He slowly and gravely read,
'You are charged here—I'm sorry to say it—

With stealing three loaves of bread.

'You look not like an offender,
   And I hope that you can show
The charge to be false. Now, tell me,
   Are you guilty of this, or no?'
A passionate burst of weeping
   Was at first her sole reply;
But she dried her eyes in a moment,
   And looked in the judge's eye.

'I will tell you just how it was, sir;
   My father and mother are dead,
And my little brothers and sisters
   Were hungry and asked me for bread.
At first I earned it for them
   By working hard all day,
But somehow, times were bad, sir,
   And the work all fell away.

'I could get no more employment;
   The weather was bitter cold;
The young ones cried and shivered
   (Little Johnny's but four years old).
So what was I to do, sir?
   I am guilty, but do not condemn;
I *took*—oh, was it *stealing*?—
   The bread to give to them.'

Every man in the court-room—
   Grey-beard and thoughtless youth—
Knew, as he looked upon her,
   That the prisoner spake the truth;

Out from their pockets came kerchiefs,
    Out from their eyes sprung tears,
And out from their old faded wallets
    Treasures hoarded for years.

The judge's face was a study,
    The strangest you ever saw,
As he cleared his throat and murmured
    Something about the *law*.
For one so learned in such matters,
    So wise in dealing with men,
He seemed on a simple question
    Sorely puzzled just then.

But no one blamed him, or wondered,
    When at last these words they heard,
'The sentence of this young prisoner
    Is, for the present deferred.'
And no one blamed him, or wondered
    When he went to her and smiled
And tenderly led from the court-room,
    Himself, the 'guilty' child.

MOTHER'S FOOL

Anonymous

I love this anonymous piece, which is extremely popular on the Internet. It talks about how a poor farmer's son becomes governor, and dwells on the fact that just knowledge is not enough—you must know how to apply that knowledge. It is not necessary that the one who tops the class will always excel.

"'Tis plain to see,' said a farmer's wife,
'These boys will make their mark in life;
They were never made to handle a hoe,
And at once to a college ought to go;
There's Fred, he's little better than a fool,
But John and Henry must go to school.'

'Well, really, wife,' quoth Farmer Brown,
As he set his mug of cider down,
'Fred does more work in a day for me
Than both his brothers do in three.
Book larnin' will never plant one's corn,
Nor hoe potatoes, sure's you're born;
Nor mend a rod of broken fence—
For my part, give me common sense.'

But his wife was bound the roost to rule,
And John and Henry were sent to school,
While Fred, of course, was left behind,
Because his mother said he had no mind.

Five years at school the students spent;
Then into business each one went.
John learned to play the flute and fiddle,
And parted his hair, of course, in the middle;
While his brother looked rather higher than he,
And hung out a sign, 'H. Brown, MD.'

Meanwhile, at home, their brother Fred
Had taken a notion into his head;
But he quietly trimmed his apple trees,
And weeded onions and planted peas,
While somehow or other, by hook or crook,

He managed to read full many a book;
Until at last his father said
He was getting 'book larnin' into his head;
'But for all that,' added Farmer Brown,
'He's the smartest boy there is in town.'

The war broke out, and Captain Fred
A hundred men to battle led,
And when the rebel flag came down,
Went marching home as General Brown.
But he went to work on the farm again,
And planted corn and sowed his grain;
He shingled the barn and mended the fence,
Till people declared he had common sense.

Now common sense was very rare,
And the State House needed a portion there;
So the 'family dunce' moved into town—
The people called him Governor Brown;
And the brothers who went to the city school
Came home to live with 'mother's fool.'

NIGHT OF THE SCORPION

Nissim Ezekiel

*Many of you may have read this poem in your CBSE or ICSE English textbooks.
It is also a great piece for elocution, especially if you want to speak something by
an Indian writer. The conflict between the peasants 'buzzing the name of God'
and the father, 'sceptic, rationalist, trying every curse and blessing', is the central
theme of this strong, narrative poem. It is a difficult piece so try it only if you
are confident about your skills. It is recommended for middle-school students.*

I remember the night my mother
was stung by a scorpion. Ten hours
of steady rain had driven him
to crawl beneath a sack of rice.
Parting with his poison—flash
of diabolic tail in the dark room—
he risked the rain again.
The peasants came like swarms of flies
and buzzed the name of God a hundred times
to paralyse the Evil One.
With candles and with lanterns
throwing giant scorpion shadows
on the mud-baked walls
they searched for him: he was not found.
They clicked their tongues.
With every movement that the scorpion made
his poison moved in Mother's blood, they said.
May he sit still, they said
May the sins of your previous birth
be burned away tonight, they said.
May your suffering decrease
the misfortunes of your next birth, they said.
May the sum of all evil
balanced in this unreal world
against the sum of good
become diminished by your pain.
May the poison purify your flesh
of desire, and your spirit of ambition,
they said, and they sat around
on the floor with my mother in the centre,
the peace of understanding on each face.

More candles, more lanterns, more neighbours,
more insects, and the endless rain.
My mother twisted through and through,
groaning on a mat.
My father, sceptic, rationalist,
trying every curse and blessing,
powder, mixture, herb and hybrid.
He even poured a little paraffin
upon the bitten toe and put a match to it.
I watched the flame feeding on my mother.
I watched the holy man perform his rites
to tame the poison with an incantation.
After twenty hours
it lost its sting.
My mother only said
Thank God the scorpion picked on me
And spared my children.

SOMEBODY'S MOTHER

Mary Dow Brine

*The poem is a touching tale about a young boy helping an old lady cross the street.
I would recommend this for anyone with a soft voice. You can use the softness of
your voice to your advantage while reciting this poem.*

The woman was old, and ragged, and gray,
And bent with the chill of a winter's day;
The streets were white with a recent snow,
And the woman's feet with age were slow.

At the crowded crossing she waited long,
Jostled aside by the careless throng
Of human beings who passed her by,
Nor heeded the glance of her anxious eye.

Down the street with laughter and shout,
Glad in the freedom of 'school let out,'
Come happy boys, like a flock of sheep,
Hailing the snow piled white and deep;
Past the woman, so old and gray,
Hastened the children on their way.

None offered a helping hand to her,
So weak and timid, afraid to stir,
Lest the carriage wheels or the horses' feet
Should trample her down in the slippery street.

At last came out of the merry troop
The gayest boy of all the group;
He paused beside her, and whispered low,
'I'll help you across, if you wish to go.'

Her aged hand on his strong young arm
She placed, and so without hurt or harm,
He guided the trembling feet along,
Proud that his own were young and strong;
Then back again to his friends he went,
His young heart happy and well content.

'She's somebody's mother, boys, you know,
For all she's agèd, and poor, and slow;
And I hope some fellow will lend a hand
To help my mother, you understand,

If ever she's poor, and old, and gray,
And her own dear boy is far away.'

'Somebody's mother' bowed low her head,
In her home that night, and the prayer she said
Was: 'God, be kind to that noble boy,
Who is somebody's son, and pride and joy.'

Faint was the voice, and worn and weak,
But the Father hears when His children speak;
Angels caught the faltering word,
And 'Somebody's Mother's' prayer was heard.

TELEVISION
Roald Dahl

An elocution contest, they say, is not complete without at least one of Roald Dahl's classics being recited. Dahl has written many brilliant poems, especially Revolting Rhymes, *a collection of fairy tales rewritten in verse. This is a popular piece from his best-selling book,* Charlie and the Chocolate Factory. *Even though this poem was written in the 1960s, it is perfectly relevant today.*

The most important thing we've learned,
So far as children are concerned,
Is never, NEVER, NEVER let
Them near your television set—
Or better still, just don't install
The idiotic thing at all.

In almost every house we've been,
We've watched them gaping at the screen.
They loll and slop and lounge about,

And stare until their eyes pop out.

(Last week in someone's place we saw
A dozen eyeballs on the floor.)
They sit and stare and stare and sit
Until they're hypnotized by it,
Until they're absolutely drunk
With all that shocking ghastly junk.

Oh yes, we know it keeps them still,
They don't climb out the window sill,
They never fight or kick or punch,
They leave you free to cook the lunch
And wash the dishes in the sink—
But did you ever stop to think,
To wonder just exactly what
This does to your beloved tot?

It rots the sense in the head!
It kills imagination dead!
It clogs and clutters up the mind!
It makes a child so dull and blind
He can no longer understand
A fantasy, a fairyland!
His brain becomes as soft as cheese!
His powers of thinking rust and freeze!
He cannot think—he only sees!

'All right!' you'll cry. 'All right!' you'll say,
'But if we take the set away,
What shall we do to entertain
Our darling children? Please explain!'
We'll answer this by asking you,

'What used the darling ones to do?

'How used they keep themselves contented
Before this monster was invented?'
Have you forgotten? Don't you know?
We'll say it very loud and slow:
THEY...USED...TO...READ! They'd READ and READ,
AND READ and READ, and then proceed
To READ some more. Great Scott! Gadzooks!
One half their lives was reading books!
The nursery shelves held books galore!
Books cluttered up the nursery floor!

And in the bedroom, by the bed,
More books were waiting to be read!
Such wondrous, fine, fantastic tales
Of dragons, gypsies, queens, and whales
And treasure isles, and distant shores
Where smugglers rowed with muffled oars,
And pirates wearing purple pants,
And sailing ships and elephants,
And cannibals crouching 'round the pot,
Stirring away at something hot.

(It smells so good, what can it be?
Good gracious, it's Penelope.)
The younger ones had Beatrix Potter
With Mr Toad, the dirty rotter,
And Squirrel Nutkin, Pigling Bland,
And Mrs Tiggy-Winkle and—
Just How The Camel Got His Hump,
And How the Monkey Lost His Rump,

And Mr Toad, and bless my soul,
There's Mr Rate and Mr Mole—
Oh, books, what books they used to know,
Those children living long ago!

So please, oh please, we beg, we pray,
Go throw your TV set away,
And in its place you can install
A lovely bookshelf on the wall.
Then fill the shelves with lots of books,
Ignoring all the dirty looks,
The screams and yells, the bites and kicks,
And children hitting you with sticks—
Fear not, because we promise you
That, in about a week or two
Of having nothing else to do,
They'll now begin to feel the need
Of having something to read.

And once they start—oh boy, oh boy!
You watch the slowly growing joy
That fills their hearts. They'll grow so keen
They'll wonder what they'd ever seen
In that ridiculous machine,
That nauseating, foul, unclean,
Repulsive television screen!
And later, each and every kid
Will love you more for what you did.

THE COOKIE THIEF

Valerie Cox

This poem is an inspirational piece that tells us, 'never assume and jump to conclusions' with people and situations. There is a surprising twist at the end, so you will need to bring in the element of surprise in your voice. I feel this would work better for girls. A trifle short and more suited for class elocution, I had to include this piece because I just love the twist at the end.

A woman was waiting at an airport one night
With several long hours before her flight
She hunted for a book in the airport shop
Bought a bag of cookies and found a place to drop
She was engrossed in her book but happened to see
That the man beside her as bold as could be
Grabbed a cookie or two from the bag between
Which she tried to ignore to avoid a scene
She munched cookies and watched the clock
As this gutsy cookie thief diminished her stock
She was getting more irritated as the minutes ticked by
Thinking 'If I wasn't so nice I'd blacken his eye'
With each cookie she took he took one too
And when only one was left she wondered what he'd do
With a smile on his face and a nervous laugh
He took the last cookie and broke it in half
He offered her half as he ate the other
She snatched it from him and thought 'Oh brother
This guy has some nerve and he's also rude
Why he didn't even show any gratitude'
She had never known when she had been so galled
And sighed with relief when her flight was called

She gathered her belongings and headed for the gate
Refusing to look back at the thieving ingrate
She boarded the plane and sank in her seat
Then sought her book which was almost complete
As she reached in her baggage she gasped with surprise
There was her bag of cookies in front of her eyes
'If mine are here' she moaned with despair
'Then the others were his and he tried to share'
'Too late to apologize she realized with grief'
That she was the rude one, the ingrate, the thief.

THE GRAY SWAN
Alice Cary

This poem, filled with sadness, is about a mother's search for her lost son. There are two distinct voices—that of the mother, filled with desperation, and that of the young sailor, with controlled emotion. The deeper the sensitivity in the two voices, the greater will be the impact.

'Oh tell me, sailor, tell me true,
Is my little lad, my Elihu,
A-sailing with your ship?'
The sailor's eyes were dim with dew,—
'Your little lad, your Elihu?'
He said, with trembling lip,—
'What little lad? What ship?'

'What little lad! as if there could be
Another such an one as he!
What little lad, do you say?

Why, Elihu, that took the sea
The moment I put him off my knee!
It was just the other day
The *Gray Swan* sailed away.'

'The, other day?' the sailor's eyes
Stood open with a great surprise,—
'The other day? the *Swan?*'
His heart began in his throat to rise.
'Ay, ay, sir, here in the cupboard lies
The jacket he had on.'
'And so your lad is gone?'

'Gone with the Swan.' 'And did she stand
With her anchor clutching hold of the sand,
For a month, and never stir?'
'Why, to be sure! I've seen from the land,
Like a lover kissing his lady's hand,
The wild sea kissing her,—
A sight to remember, sir.'

'But, my good mother, do you know
All this was twenty years ago?
I stood on the *Gray Swan's* deck,
And to that lad I saw you throw,
Taking it off, as it might be, so!
The kerchief from your neck.'
'Ay, and he'll bring it back!'

'And did the little lawless lad
That has made you sick and made you sad,
Sail with the *Gray Swan's crew?*'
'Lawless! The man is going mad!

The best boy ever mother had,—
Be sure he sailed with the crew!
What would you have him do?

'And he has never written line,
Nor sent you word, nor made you sign
To say he was alive?'
'Hold! if 't was wrong, the wrong is mine;
Besides, he may be in the brine,
And could he write from the grave?
Tut, man! What would you have?'

'Gone twenty years,—a long, long cruise,—
'T was wicked thus your love to abuse;
But if the lad still live,
And come back home, think you you can
Forgive him?'—'Miserable man,
You're mad as the sea,—you rave,—
What have I to forgive?'

The sailor twitched his shirt so blue,
And from within his bosom drew
The kerchief. She was wild.
'My God! My Father! Is it true?
My little lad, my Elihu!
My blessed boy, my child!
My dead, my living child!'

THE QUEEN'S RIVAL

Sarojini Naidu

This poem is from **The Golden Threshold**, *written in 1905. Quite unlike Sarojini Naidu's other poems, this is written in the simple couplet form, and tells the story of a beautiful queen, bored of her looks, who asks her king to find someone that rivals her beauty. Be a little careful with the pronunciation of some words; your voice should at times be heraldic (when describing the palace or when you are the king) and slightly sorrowful (when you are the queen).*

I

Queen Gulnaar sat on her ivory bed,
Around her countless treasures were spread;

Her chamber walls were richly inlaid
With agate, porphyry, onyx and jade;

The tissues that veiled her delicate breast,
Glowed with the hues of a lapwing's crest;

But still she gazed in her mirror and sighed
'O King, my heart is unsatisfied.'

King Feroz bent from his ebony seat:
'Is thy least desire unfulfilled, O Sweet?

'Let thy mouth speak and my life be spent
To clear the sky of thy discontent.'

'I tire of my beauty, I tire of this
Empty splendour and shadowless bliss;

'With none to envy and none gainsay,
No savour or salt hath my dream or day.'

Queen Gulnaar sighed like a murmuring rose:
'Give me a rival, O King Feroz.'

II

King Feroz spoke to his Chief Vizier:
'Lo! ere tomorrow's dawn be here,

'Send forth my messengers over the sea,
To seek seven beautiful brides for me;

'Radiant of feature and regal of mien,
Seven handmaids meet for the Persian Queen'...

Seven new moon tides at the Vesper call,
King Feroz led to Queen Gulnaar's hall

A young queen eyed like the morning star:
'I bring thee a rival, O Queen Gulnaar.'

But still she gazed in her mirror and sighed:
'O King, my heart is unsatisfied.'

Seven queens shone round her ivory bed,
Like seven soft gems on a silken thread,

Like seven fair lamps in a royal tower,
Like seven bright petals of Beauty's flower

Queen Gulnaar sighed like a murmuring rose
'Where is my rival, O King Feroz?'

III

When spring winds wakened the mountain floods,
And kindled the flame of the tulip buds,

When bees grew loud and the days grew long,

And the peach groves thrilled to the oriole's song,

Queen Gulnaar sat on her ivory bed,
Decking with jewels her exquisite head;

And still she gazed in her mirror and sighed:
'O King, my heart is unsatisfied.'

Queen Gulnaar's daughter two spring times old,
In blue robes bordered with tassels of gold,

Ran to her knee like a wildwood fay,
And plucked from her hand the mirror away.

Quickly she set on her own light curls
Her mother's fillet with fringes of pearls;

Quickly she turned with a child's caprice
And pressed on the mirror a swift, glad kiss.

Queen Gulnaar laughed like a tremulous rose:
'Here is my rival, O King Feroz.'

THE TEACHER'S 'IF'

R. J. Gale

Many of you may have read and recited Rudyard Kipling's classic poem 'If'. While that poem is very popular for elocution contests, here is the teacher's version of that immortal poem. It is an ideal piece to recite on Teacher's Day or any special occasion where you would like to appreciate your teachers.

If you can take your dreams into the classroom,
And always make them part of each day's work—

If you can face the countless petty problems
Nor turn from them nor ever try to shirk—
If you can live so that the child you work with
Deep in his heart knows you to be a man—
If you can take 'I can't' from out his language
And put in place a vigorous 'I can'—

If you can take Love with you to the classroom,
And yet on Firmness never shut the door—
If you can teach a child the love of Nature
So that he helps himself to all her store—
If you can teach him life is what we make it,
That he himself can be his only bar—
If you can tell him something of the heavens,
Or something of the wonder of a star—

If you, with simple bits of truth and honour,
His better self occasionally reach—
And yet not overdo nor have him dub you
As one who is inclined to ever preach—
If you impart to him a bit of liking
For all the wondrous things we find in print—
Yet have him understand that to be happy,
Play, exercise, fresh air he must not stint—

If you can give of all the best that's in you,
And in the giving always happy be—
If you can find the good that's hidden somewhere
Deep in the heart of every child you see—
If you can do these things and all the others
That teachers everywhere do every day—
You're in the work that you were surely meant for;
Take hold of it! Know it's your place and stay!

TOMMY'S PRAYER

John F. Nicholls

This poem is set at the time of the industrial revolution in England, in the mid-nineteenth century. It's a soul-searching piece, with a punch at the end. An ideal way to deliver this one would be to begin in softer tones and end with a booming, hope-filled, happy voice.

In a dark and dismal alley where the sunshine never came,
Dwelt a little lad named Tommy, sickly, delicate, and lame;
He had never yet been healthy, but had lain since he was
     born
Dragging out his weak existence well nigh hopeless and
     forlorn.

He was six, was little Tommy, 'twas just five years ago
Since his drunken mother dropped him, and the babe was
     crippled so.
He had never known the comfort of a mother's tender care,
But her cruel blows and curses made his pain still worse to
     bear.

There he lay within the cellar, from the morning till the
     night,
Starved, neglected, cursed, ill-treated, nought to make his
     dull life bright;
Not a single friend to love him, not a loving thing to love—
For he knew not of a Saviour, or a heaven up above.

'Twas a quiet, summer evening, and the alley, too, was
     still;
Tommy's little heart was sinking, and he felt so lonely, till,

Floating up the quiet alley, wafted inwards from the street,
Came the sound of someone singing, sounding, oh! so clear
     and sweet.

Eagerly did Tommy listen as the singing came—
Oh! that he could see the singer! How he wished he wasn't
     lame.
Then he called and shouted loudly, till the singer heard the
     sound,
And on noting whence it issued, soon the little cripple
     found.

'Twas a maiden rough and rugged, hair unkempt, and
     naked feet,
All her garments torn and ragged, her appearance far from
     neat;
'So yer called me,' said the maiden, 'wonder wot yer wants
     o' me;
Most folks call me Singing Jessie; wot may your name
     chance to be?'

'My name's Tommy; I'm a cripple, and I want to hear you
     sing,
For it makes me feel so happy—sing me something,
     anything,'
Jessie laughed, and answered smiling, 'I can't stay here very
     long,
But I'll sing a hymn to please you, wot I calls the 'Glory Song.'

Then she sang to him of heaven, pearly gates, and streets of
     gold,
Where the happy angel children are not starved or nipped
     with cold;

But where happiness and gladness never can decrease or
  end,
And where kind and loving Jesus is their Sovereign and
  their Friend.

Oh! how Tommy's eyes did glisten as he drank in every
  word
As it fell from 'Singing Jessie'—was it true, what he had
  heard?
And so anxiously he asked her, 'Is there really such a
  place?'
And a tear began to trickle down his pallid little face.

'Tommy, you're a little heathen; why, it's up beyond the sky,
And if yer will love the Saviour, yer shall go there when yer die.'
'Then,' said Tommy, 'tell me, Jessie, how can I the Saviour
  love,
When I'm down in this 'ere cellar, and He's up in heaven
  above?'

So the little ragged maiden who had heard at Sunday
  School
All about the way to heaven, and the Christian's golden
  rule,
Taught the little cripple Tommy how to love, and how to
  pray,
Then she sang a 'Song of Jesus,' kissed his cheek and went
  away.

Tommy lay within the cellar which had grown so dark and
  cold,
Thinking all about the children in the streets of shining
  gold;

And he heeded not the darkness of that damp and chilly
    room,
For the joy in Tommy's bosom could disperse the deepest
    gloom.

'Oh! if I could only see it,' thought the cripple, as he lay,
'Jessie said that Jesus listens and I think I'll try and pray';
So he put his hands together, and he closed his little eyes,
And in accents weak, yet earnest, sent this message to the
    skies:—

'Gentle Jesus, please forgive me as I didn't know afore,
That yer cared for little cripples who is weak and very poor,
And I never heard of heaven till that Jessie came today
And told me all about it, so I wants to try and pray.'

'Yer can see me, can't yer, Jesus? Jessie told me that yer
    could,
And I somehow must believe it, for it seems so prime and
    good;
And she told me if I loved you, I should see yer when I
    die,
In the bright and happy heaven that is up beyond the sky.'

'Lord, I'm only just a cripple, and I'm no use here below,
For I heard my mother whisper, she'd be glad if I could go;
And I'm cold and hungry sometimes; and I feel so lonely,
    too,
Can't yer take me, gentle Jesus, up to heaven along with
    you?'

'Oh! I'd be so good and patient, and I'd never cry or fret,
And your kindness to me, Jesus, I would surely not forget;

I would love you all I know of, and would never make a
    noise—
Can't you find me just a corner, where I'll watch the other
    boys?'

'Oh! I think yer'll do it, Jesus, something seems to tell me so,
For I feel so glad and happy, and I do so want to go,
How I long to see yer, Jesus, and the children all so bright!
Come and fetch me, won't yer, Jesus? Come and fetch me
    home tonight!'

Tommy ceased his supplication, he had told his soul's
    desire,
And he waited for the answer till his head began to tire;
Then he turned towards his corner and lay huddled in a
    heap,
Closed his little eyes so gently, and was quickly fast asleep.

Oh, I wish that every scoffer could have seen his little face
As he lay there in the corner, in that damp, and noisome
    place;
For his countenance was shining like an angel's, fair and
    bright,
And it seemed to fill the cellar with a holy, heavenly light.

He had only heard of Jesus from a ragged singing girl,
He might well have wondered, pondered, till his brain
    began to whirl;
But he took it as she told it, and believed it then and there,
Simply trusting in the Saviour, and his kind and tender care.

In the morning, when the mother came to wake her
    crippled boy,

She discovered that his features wore a look of sweetest joy,
And she shook him somewhat roughly, but the cripple's face
    was cold—
He had gone to join the children in the streets of shining
    gold.

Tommy's prayer had soon been answered, and the Angel
    Death had come
To remove him from his cellar, to his bright and heavenly
    home
Where sweet comfort, joy, and gladness never can decrease
    or end,
And where Jesus reigns eternally, his Sovereign and his
    Friend.

TROUBLE IN THE 'AMEN CORNER'
T. C. Harbaugh

*A fun poem, with a sad undertone, about a sweet old man who continues to sing
in the church choir though his voice is 'cracked and broken', and how the people
in church are trying to get rid of him. Make full use of your voice, speaking in
a softer, more tender tone when referring to the old man.*

'Twas a stylish congregation, that of Theophrastus Brown,
And its organ was the finest and the biggest in the town,
And the chorus—all the papers favourably commented on
    it,
For 'twas said each female member had a forty-dollar
    bonnet.

Now in the 'amen corner' of the church sat Brother Eyer,

Who persisted every Sabbath-day in singing with the choir;
He was poor but genteel-looking, and his heart as snow was
    white,
And his old face beamed with sweetness when he sang with
    all his might.

His voice was cracked and broken, age had touched his
    vocal chords,
And nearly every Sunday he would mispronounce the words
Of the hymns, and 'twas no wonder, he was old and nearly
    blind,
And the choir rattling onward always left him far behind.

The chorus stormed and blustered, Brother Eyer sang too slow,
And then he used the tunes in vogue a hundred years ago;
At last the storm-cloud burst, and the church was told, in fine,
That the brother must stop singing, or the choir would resign.

Then the pastor called together in the vestry-room one day
Seven influential members who subscribe more than they pay,
And having asked God's guidance in a printed pray'r or two,
They put their heads together to determine what to do.

They debated, thought, suggested, till at last 'dear Brother
    York,'
Who last winter made a million on a sudden rise in pork,
Rose and moved that a committee wait at once on Brother Eyer,
And proceed to rake him lively 'for disturbin' of the choir.'

Said he: 'In that 'ere organ I've invested quite a pile,
And we'll sell it if we cannot worship in the latest style;
Our Philadelphy tenor tells me 'tis the hardest thing
Fer to make God understand him when the brother tries to
    sing.

'We've got the biggest organ, the best-dressed choir in town,
We pay the steepest sal'ry to our pastor, Brother Brown;
But if we must humour ignorance because it's blind and
    old—
If the choir's to be pestered, I will seek another fold.'

Of course the motion carried, and one day a coach and
    four,
With the latest style of driver, rattled up to Eyer's door;
And the sleek, well-dress'd committee, Brothers Sharkey,
    York and Lamb,
As they crossed the humble portal took good care to miss
    the jamb.

They found the choir's great trouble sitting in his old arm chair,
And the Summer's golden sunbeams lay upon his thin
    white hair;
He was singing 'Rock of Ages' in a cracked voice and low
But the angels understood him, 'twas all he cared to know.

Said York: 'We're here, dear brother, with the vestry's
    approbation
To discuss a little matter that affects the congregation';
'And the choir, too,' said Sharkey, giving Brother York a nudge,
'And the choir, too!' he echoed with the graveness of a judge.

'It was the understanding when we bargained for the chorus
That it was to relieve us, that is, do the singing for us;
If we rupture the agreement, it is very plain, dear brother,
It will leave our congregation and be gobbled by another.

'We don't want any singing except that what we've bought!
The latest tunes are all the rage; the old ones stand for naught;

And so we have decided—are you list'ning, Brother Eyer?—
That you'll have to stop your singin' for it flurrytates the choir.'

The old man slowly raised his head, a sign that he did hear,
And on his cheek the trio caught the glitter of a tear;
His feeble hands pushed back the locks white as the silky snow,
As he answered the committee in a voice both sweet and low:

'I've sung the psalms of David nearly eighty years,' said he;
'They've been my staff and comfort all along life's dreary
    way;
I'm sorry I disturb the choir, perhaps I'm doing wrong;
But when my heart is filled with praise, I can't keep back a
    song.

'I wonder if beyond the tide that's breaking at my feet,
In the far-off heav'nly temple, where the Master I shall greet—
Yes, I wonder when I try to sing the songs of God up
    high'r,
If the angel band will church me for disturbing heaven's choir.'

A silence filled the little room; the old man bowed his
    head;
The carriage rattled on again, but Brother Eyer was dead!
Yes, dead! his hand had raised the veil the future hangs
    before us,
And the Master dear had called him to the everlasting chorus.

The choir missed him for a while, but he was soon forgot,
A few churchgoers watched the door; the old man entered not.
Far away, his voice no longer cracked, he sang his heart's
    desires,
Where there are no church committees and no fashionable
    choirs!

UNAWARES

Emma A. Lent

We have heard this story in so many different forms, and here it is narrated as a poem: of a young woman preparing for God to visit her home, expecting someone dressed like a king, not realizing that he had already visited her thrice in disguise. An inspirational piece, it teaches us to be respectful and kind to all, no matter how wealthy and famous or how poor and insignificant one is.

M I D D L E   S C H O O L

They said, 'The Master is coming
　　To honour the town today,
And none can tell at what house or home
　　The Master will choose to stay.'
And I thought while my heart beat wildly,
　　What if He should come to mine,
How would I strive to entertain
　　And honour the Guest Divine!

And straight I turned to toiling
　　To make my house more neat;
I swept, and polished, and garnished.
　　And decked it with blossoms sweet.
I was troubled for fear the Master
　　Might come ere my work was done,
And I hasted and worked the faster,
　　And watched the hurrying sun.

But right in the midst of my duties
　　A woman came to my door;
She had come to tell me her sorrows
　　And my comfort and aid to implore,
And I said, 'I cannot listen

Nor help you any, today;
I have greater things to attend to.'
    And the pleader turned away.

But soon there came another—
    A cripple, thin, pale and gray—
And said, 'Oh, let me stop and rest
    A while in your house, I pray!
I have travelled far since morning,
    I am hungry, and faint, and weak;
My heart is full of misery,
    And comfort and help I seek.'

And I cried, 'I am grieved and sorry,
    But I cannot help you today.
I look for a great and noble Guest,'
    And the cripple went away;
And the day wore onward swiftly—
    And my task was nearly done,
And a prayer was ever in my heart
    That the Master to me might come.

And I thought I would spring to meet Him,
    And serve him with utmost care,
When a little child stood by me
    With a face so sweet and fair—
Sweet, but with marks of teardrops—
    And his clothes were tattered and old;
A finger was bruised and bleeding,
    And his little bare feet were cold.

And I said, 'I'm sorry for you—
    You are sorely in need of care;

But I cannot stop to give it,
    You must hasten otherwhere.'
And at the words, a shadow
    Swept o'er his blue-veined brow,—
'Someone will feed and clothe you, dear,
    But I am too busy now.'

At last the day was ended,
    And my toil was over and done;
My house was swept and garnished—
    And I watched in the dark—alone.
Watched—but no footfall sounded,
    No one paused at my gate;
No one entered my cottage door;
    I could only pray—and wait.

I waited till night had deepened,
    And the Master had not come.
'He has entered some other door,' I said,
    'And gladdened some other home!'
My labour had been for nothing,
    And I bowed my head and I wept,
My heart was sore with longing—
    Yet—in spite of it all—I slept.

Then the Master stood before me,
    And his face was grave and fair;
'Three times today I came to your door,
    And craved your pity and care;
Three times you sent me onward,
    Unhelped and uncomforted;
And the blessing you might have had was lost,
    And your chance to serve has fled.'

'O Lord, dear Lord, forgive me!
      How could I know it was Thee?'
My very soul was shamed and bowed
      In the depths of humility.
And He said, 'The sin is pardoned,
      But the blessing is lost to thee;
For comforting not the least of Mine
      You have failed to comfort Me.'

HOW THEY BROUGHT THE GOOD NEWS FROM GHENT TO AIX

Robert Browning

Some poems work just because they tell such a good story. This one is a classic example. This fast-paced poem should be recited in a way that brings out the urgency and speed at which the riders are riding. However, since it is such a popular piece, make sure that someone else in class does not choose it too!

I sprang to the stirrup, and Joris, and he;
I galloped, Dirck galloped, we galloped all three;
'Good speed!' cried the watch, as the gate-bolts undrew;
'Speed!' echoed the wall to us galloping through;
Behind shut the postern, the lights sank to rest,
And into the midnight we galloped abreast.

Not a word to each other; we kept the great pace
Neck by neck, stride by stride, never changing our place;
I turned in my saddle and made its girths tight,
Then shortened each stirrup, and set the pique right,
Rebuckled the cheek-strap, chained slacker the bit,
Nor galloped less steadily Roland a whit.

'Twas moonset at starting; but while we drew near
Lokeren, the cocks crew and twilight dawned clear;
At Boom, a great yellow star came out to see;
At Düffeld, 'twas morning as plain as could be;
And from Mecheln church-steeple we heard the half-chime,
So Joris broke silence with 'Yet there is time!'

At Aerschot, up leaped of a sudden the sun,
And against him the cattle stood black every one,

To stare through the mist at us galloping past,
And I saw my stout galloper Roland at last,
With resolute shoulders, each butting away
The haze, as some bluff river headland its spray:

And his low head and crest, just one sharp ear bent back
For my voice, and the other pricked out on his track;
And one eye's black intelligence,—ever that glance
O'er its white edge at me, his own master, askance!
And the thick heavy spume-flakes which aye and anon
His fierce lips shook upwards in galloping on.

By Hasselt, Dirck groaned; and cried Joris, 'Stay spur!
Your Roos galloped bravely, the fault's not in her,
We'll remember at Aix'—for one heard the quick wheeze
Of her chest, saw the stretched neck and staggering knees,
And sunk tail, and horrible heave of the flank,
As down on her haunches she shuddered and sank.

So we were left galloping, Joris and I,
Past Looz and past Tongres, no cloud in the sky;
The broad sun above laughed a pitiless laugh,
'Neath our feet broke the brittle bright stubble like chaff;
Till over by Dalhem a dome-spire sprang white,
And 'Gallop,' gasped Joris, 'for Aix is in sight!'

'How they'll greet us!'—and all in a moment his roan
Rolled neck and croup over, lay dead as a stone;
And there was my Roland to bear the whole weight
Of the news which alone could save Aix from her fate,
With his nostrils like pits full of blood to the brim,
And with circles of red for his eye-sockets' rim.

Then I cast loose my buffcoat, each holster let fall,
Shook off both my jack-boots, let go belt and all,
Stood up in the stirrup, leaned, patted his ear,
Called my Roland his pet-name, my horse without peer;
Clapped my hands, laughed and sang, any noise, bad or good,
Till at length into Aix Roland galloped and stood.

And all I remember is, friends flocking round
As I sat with his head 'twixt my knees on the ground;
And no voice but was praising this Roland of mine,
As I poured down his throat our last measure of wine,
Which (the burgesses voted by common consent)
Was no more than his due who brought good news from
    Ghent.

WHO

Sri Aurobindo

Sri Aurobindo gave the world a vision of a new human existence based on the power of the spirit. If you can handle serious themes, and have a powerful voice, try this. Unfortunately, not the kind of poem I would have attempted when I was in school, as I was one of the naughty ones!

In the blue of the sky, in the green of the forest,
Whose is the hand that has painted the glow?
When the winds were asleep in the womb of the ether,
Who was it roused them and bade them to blow?

He is lost in the heart, in the cavern of Nature,
He is found in the brain where He builds up the thought:
In the pattern and bloom of the flowers He is woven,

In the luminous net of the stars He is caught.

In the strength of a man, in the beauty of woman,
In the laugh of a boy, in the blush of a girl;
The hand that sent Jupiter spinning through heaven,
Spends all its cunning to fashion a curl.

There are His works and His veils and His shadows;
But where is He then? by what name is He known?
Is He Brahma or Vishnu? a man or a woman?
Bodies or bodiless? twin or alone?

We have love for a boy who is dark and resplendent,
A woman is lord of us, naked and fierce.
We have seen Him a-muse on the snow of the mountains,
We have watched Him at work in the heart of the spheres.

We will tell the whole world of His ways and His cunning;
He has rapture of torture and passion and pain;
He delights in our sorrow and drives us to weeping,
Then lures with His joy and His beauty again.

All music is only the sound of His laughter,
All beauty the smile of His passionate bliss;
Our lives are His heartbeats, our rapture the bridal
Of Radha and Krishna, our love is their kiss.

He is strength that is loud in the blare of the trumpets,
And He rides in the car and He strikes in the spears;
He slays without stint and is full of compassion;
He wars for the world and its ultimate years.

In the sweep of the worlds, in the surge of the ages,
Ineffable, mighty, majestic and pure,

Beyond the last pinnacle seized by the thinker
He is throned in His seats that for ever endure.

The Master of man and his infinite Lover,
He is close to our hearts, had we vision to see;
We are blind with our pride and the pomp of our passions,
We are bound in our thoughts where we hold ourselves free.

It is He in the sun who is ageless and deathless,
And into the midnight His shadow is thrown;
When darkness was blind and engulfed within darkness,
He was seated within it immense and alone.

Kamala Das

Kamala Surayya was a leading poet from Kerala. She wrote her fiery English poetry under the name Kamala Das. In this poem, she is giving voice to her uniquely Indian womanhood and sharing her experiences, good or bad, as a woman. It is an ideal piece for a young lady in senior school. It needs to be spoken with conviction, so a strong voice is a must.

I don't know politics but I know the names
Of those in power, and can repeat them like
Days of week, or names of months, beginning with Nehru.
I am Indian, very brown, born in Malabar,
I speak three languages, write in two, dream in one.
Don't write in English, they said,
English is not your mother-tongue.
Why not leave me alone, critics, friends, visiting cousins,
Every one of you?
Why not let me speak in any language I like?
The language I speak becomes mine,
Its distortions, its queernesses, all mine, mine alone.
It is half English, half Indian, funny perhaps, but it is
    honest,
It is as human as I am human, don't you see?
It voices my joys, my longings, my
Hopes, and it is useful to me as cawing
Is to crows or roaring to the lions,
It is human speech, the speech of the mind
That is here and not there,
A mind that sees and hears and is aware.
Not the deaf, blind speech of trees in storm

Or of monsoon clouds or of rain or the
Incoherent mutterings of the blazing funeral pyre.
I was child, and later they told me I grew,
For I became tall, my limbs swelled.
Then... I wore a shirt and my brother's trousers,
Cut my hair short and ignored my womanliness.
Dress in sarees, be girl, be wife, they said.
Be embroiderer, be cook, be a quarreller with servants.
Fit in. Oh, belong, cried the categorizers.
Don't sit on walls or peep in through our lace-draped
    windows.
Be Amy, or be Kamala.
Or, better still, be Madhavikutty.
It is time to choose a name, a role.
Don't play pretending games.
Don't play at schizophrenia or be a nympho.
Don't cry embarrassingly loud when jilted in love...
I met a man, loved him.
Call him not by any name,
He is every man who wants a woman,
Just as I am every woman who seeks love.
In him...the hungry haste of rivers,
In me...the oceans' tireless waiting.
Who are you? I ask each and everyone,
The answer is, it is I.
Anywhere and everywhere,
I see the one who calls himself I. In this world,
He is tightly packed like the sword in its sheath.
It is I who drink lonely drinks at twelve, midnight,
In hotels of strange towns, it is I who laugh,
It is I who make love and then, feel shame,

It is I who lie dying with a rattle in my throat.
I am sinner, I am saint.
am the beloved and the betrayed.
I have no joys that are not yours,
No aches which are not yours.
I too call myself I.

IN THE SIGNAL BOX: A STATIONMASTER'S STORY
George R. Sims

Sims was a prolific writer, dramatist and poet. Of his many poems, I particularly like this one. It is the story of a stationmaster who chose to do his duty of protecting the lives of passengers on an oncoming train over rescuing his son stranded on the train tracks. By doing his duty he not only saved the train but his son was saved too. An uncommon piece, it might work to your advantage if you like telling a story.

Yes, it's a quiet station, but it suits me well enough;
I want a bit of the smooth now, for I've had my share o' rough.
This berth that the company gave me, they gave as the
    work was light;
I was never fit for the signals after one awful night,
I'd been in the box from a younker, and I'd never felt the strain
Of the lives at my right hand's mercy in every passing train.
One day there was something happened, and it made my
    nerves go queer,
And it's all through that as you find me the stationmaster
    here.
I was on at the box down yonder—that's where we turn the
    mails,
And specials, and fast expresses, on to the centre rails;

The side's for the other traffic—the luggage and local slows.
It was rare hard work at Christmas, when double the traffic
grows.
I've been in the box down yonder nigh sixteen hours a day,
Till my eyes grew dim and heavy, and my thoughts went all
astray;
But I've worked the points half-sleeping—and once I slept
outright,
Till the roar of the Limited woke me, and I nearly died
with fright.

Then I thought of the lives in peril, and what might have
been their fate
Had I sprung to the points that evening a tenth of a tick
too late;
And a cold and ghastly shiver ran icily through my frame
As I fancied the public clamor, the trial, and bitter shame.
I could see the bloody wreckage—I could see the mangled
slain—
And the picture was seared for ever, blood-red, on my
heated brain.
That moment my nerve was shattered, for I couldn't shut
out the thought
Of the lives I held in my keeping, and the ruin that might
be wrought.

That night in our little cottage, as I kissed our sleeping
child,
My wife looked up from her sewing, and told me, as she
smiled,
That Johnny had made his mind up—he'd be a pointsman,
too.

'He says when he's big, like daddy, he'll work in the box
     with you.'
I frowned, for my heart was heavy, and my wife she saw
     the look;
Lord bless you! My little Alice could read me like a book.
I'd to tell her of what had happened, and I said that I must
     leave,
For a pointsman's arm ain't trusty when terror lurks in his
     sleeve.

But she cheered me up in a minute, and that night, ere we
     went to sleep,
She made me give her a promise, which I swore that I'd
     always keep—
It was always to do my duty. 'Do that, and then, come what
     will,
You'll have no worry.' said Alice, 'if things go well or ill.
There's something that always tells us the thing that we
     ought to do'—
My wife was a bit religious, and in with the chapel crew.
But I knew she was talking reason, and I said to myself,
     says I,
'I won't give in like a coward, it's a scare that'll soon go by.'

Now, the very next day the missus had to go to the market
     town;
She'd the Christmas things to see to, and she wanted to buy
     a gown.
She'd be gone for a spell, for the Parley didn't come back till
     eight,
And I knew, on a Christmas Eve, too, the trains would be
     extra late.

So she settled to leave me Johnny, and then she could turn
    the key—
For she'd have some parcels to carry, and the boy would be
    safe with me.
He was five, was our little Johnny, and quiet, and nice, and
    good—
He was mad to go with daddy, and I'd often promised he
    should.

It was noon when the missus started,—her train went by
    my box;
She could see, as she passed my window, her darling's curly
    locks,
I lifted him up to mammy, and he kissed his little hand,
Then sat, like a mouse, in the corner, and thought it was
    fairyland.
But somehow I fell a-thinking of a scene that would not
    fade,
Of how I had slept on duty, until I grew afraid;
For the thought would weigh upon me, one day I might
    come to lie
In a felon's cell for the slaughter of those I had doomed to
    die.

The fit that had come upon me, like a hideous nightmare
    seemed,
Till I rubbed my eyes and started like a sleeper who has
    dreamed.
For a time the box had vanished—I'd worked like a mere
    machine—
My mind had been on the wander, and I'd neither heard
    nor seen,

With a start I thought of Johnny, and I turned the boy to
    seek,
Then I uttered a groan of anguish, for my lips refused to
    speak;
There had flashed such a scene of horror swift on my
    startled sight
That it curdled my blood in terror and sent my red lips
    white.

It was all in one awful moment—I saw that the boy was
    lost:
He had gone for a toy, I fancied, some child from a train
    had tossed;
The local was easing slowly to stop at the station here,
And the limited mail was coming, and I had the line to
    clear.
I could hear the roar of the engine, I could almost feel its
    breath,
And right on the centre metals stood my boy in the jaws of
    death;
On came the fierce fiend, tearing straight for the centre
    line,
And the hand that must wreck or save it, O merciful God,
    was mine!

'Twas a hundred lives or Johnny's. O Heaven! What could I
    do?—
Up to God's ear that moment a wild, fierce question
    flew—
'What shall I do, O Heaven?' and sudden and loud and
    clear

On the wind came the words, 'Your duty,' borne to my
    listening ear.
Then I set my teeth, and my breathing was fierce and short
    and quick.
'My boy!' I cried, but he heard not; and then I went blind
    and sick;
The hot black smoke of the engine came with a rush
    before,
I turned the mail to the centre, and by it flew with a roar.

Then I sank on my knees in horror, and hid my ashen
    face—
I had given my child to Heaven; his life was a hundred's
    grace.
Had I held my hand a moment, I had hurled the flying
    mail
To shatter the creeping local that stood on the other rail!
Where is my boy, my darling? O God! Let me hide my
    eyes.
How can I look—his father—on that which there mangled
    lies?
That voice!—O merciful Heaven!—'tis the child's, and he
    calls my name!
I hear, but I cannot see him, for my eyes are filled with
    flame.

I knew no more that night, sir, for I fell, as I heard the
    boy;
The place reeled round, and I fainted,—swooned with the
    sudden joy.
But I heard on the Christmas morning, when I woke in my
    own warm bed

With Alice's arms around me, and a strange wild dream in
my head,
That she'd come by the early local, being anxious about the
lad,
And had seen him there on the metals, and the sight nigh
drove her mad—
She had seen him just as the engine of the Limited closed
my view,
And she leapt on the line and saved him just as the mail
dashed through.
She was back in the train in a second, and both were safe
and sound;
The moment they stopped at the station she ran here, and I
was found
With my eyes like a madman's glaring, and my face a
ghastly white:
I heard the boy, and I fainted, and I hadn't my wits that
night.
Who told me to do my duty? What voice was that on the
wind?
Was it fancy that brought it to me? or were there God's lips
behind?
If I hadn't 'a' done my duty—had I ventured to disobey—
My bonny boy and his mother might have died by my
hand that day.

PROGRESS OF MADNESS (THE CAPTIVE)

Matthew G. Lewis

This is an ideal piece for someone who can emote in a strong, passionate and appealing manner. It is an extremely tough piece to conquer, especially because you cannot use your hands too much to express the 'madness' of the captive. You need to tell the story using just your voice, your face and your eyes. This is also one of my most favourite poems!

Stay Jailer, stay, and hear my woe!
　　She is not mad who kneels to thee,
For what I am now too well I know,
　　And what I was, and what should be.
I'll rave no more in proud despair;
　　My language shall be mild, 'though sad:
But yet I'll truly swear,
　　I am not mad! I am not mad!

My tyrant husband forged the tale,
　　Which chains me in this dreary cell:
My fate unknown my friends bewail—
　　Oh! Jailer, haste that fate to tell!
Oh! Haste my father's heart to cheer:
　　His heart at once 'twill grieve and glad
To know, though a captive here,
　　I am not mad! I am not mad!

He smiles in scorn, and turns the key!
　　He quits the grate! I knelt in vain!—
His glimmering lamp still...still I see!—
　　'Tis gone...and all is gloom again!

Cold, bitter cold!—no warmth!—no light!—
    Life, all thy comforts once I had;
Yet, here I'm chained this freezing night
    Although not mad! No, (no, no) no! not mad!

'Tis sure some dream! Some vision vain!—
    What? I, the child of rank and wealth,
Am I the wretch who clanks this chain,
    Bereft of freedom, friends and health?
Ah! While I dwell on blessings fled,
    Which never more my heart must glad,
How aches my heart! How burns my head!—
    But 'tis not mad; no 'tis not mad.

Hast thou, my child, forgot ere this
    A mother's face, a mother's tongue?
She'll ne'er forget your parting kiss,
    Nor round her neck how fast you clung:
Nor how you with me you sued to stay,
    Nor how that suit your sire forbade;
Nor how... I'll drive these thoughts away;
    They'll make me mad! They'll make me mad!

His rosy lips, how sweet they smiled!
    His mild blue eyes, how bright they shone!
None ever bore a lovelier child!—
    And art thou now forever gone,
And must I never see thee more,
    My pretty, pretty, pretty lad?
I will be free! Unbar this door!
    I am not mad! I am not mad!

Oh! Hark!—What means those yells and cries?

His chain some furious madman breaks!—
He comes!—I see his glaring eyes!—
    Now, now my dungeon grate he shakes!
Help, help!—He's gone!—Oh! Fearful woe,
    Such screams to hear, such sights to see!
My brain, my brain!—I know, I know,
    I am not mad...but soon shall be!

Yes! Soon!—For lo yon' while I speak...
    Mark, how yon daemon's eye-balls glare!—
He sees me!—Now with dreadful shriek
    He whirls a serpent high in air!—
Horror!—The reptile strikes his tooth
    Deep in my heart so crushed and sad!—
Ae, laugh, ye fiends!—I feel the truth!
    Your task is done!—I'm mad! I'm mad!

THE CREMATION OF SAM MCGEE

Robert William Service

This poem was published in 1907 in a collection called Songs of a Sourdough.
Service based the piece on the places he saw, the people he met, and the stories he heard in and around the frontier town of Whitehorse, Yukon, Canada. You will love its combination of dark humour, adventure, and its captivating descriptions of the lives of prospectors (men who searched for gold along the banks of the river Yukon). Say it like a story, making good use of your voice and using the stage whisper to good effect.

There are strange things done in the midnight sun
    By the men who moil for gold;

The Arctic trails have their secret tales
  That would make your blood run cold;
The Northern Lights have seen queer sights,
  But the queerest they ever did see
Was that night on the marge of Lake Lebarge
  I cremated Sam McGee.

Now Sam McGee was from Tennessee, where the cotton
  blooms and blows.
Why he left his home in the South to roam 'round the Pole,
  God only knows.
He was always cold, but the land of gold seemed to hold
  him like a spell;
Though he'd often say in his homely way that he'd 'sooner
  live in hell'.

On a Christmas Day we were mushing our way over the
  Dawson trail.
Talk of your cold! Through the parka's fold it stabbed like a
  driven nail.
If our eyes we'd close, then the lashes froze till sometimes
  we couldn't see;
It wasn't much fun, but the only one to whimper was Sam
  McGee.

And that very night, as we lay packed tight in our robes
  beneath the snow,
And the dogs were fed, and the stars o'erhead were dancing
  heel and toe,
He turned to me, and 'Cap,' says he, 'I'll cash in this trip, I
  guess;
And if I do, I'm asking that you won't refuse my last request.'

Well, he seemed so low that I couldn't say no; then he says
    with a sort of moan:
'It's the cursed cold, and it's got right hold till I'm chilled
    clean through to the bone.
Yet it ain't being dead—it's my awful dread of the icy grave
    that pains;
So I want you to swear that, foul or fair, you'll cremate my
    last remains.'

A pal's last need is a thing to heed, so I swore I would not
    fail;
And we started on at the streak of dawn; but God! He
    looked ghastly pale.
He crouched on the sleigh, and he raved all day of his
    home in Tennessee;
And before nightfall a corpse was all that was left of Sam
    McGee.

There wasn't a breath in that land of death, and I hurried,
    horror-driven,
With a corpse half hid that I couldn't get rid, because of a
    promise given;
It was lashed to the sleigh, and it seemed to say:
'You may tax your brawn and brains,
But you promised true, and it's up to you to cremate those
    last remains.'

Now a promise made is a debt unpaid, and the trail has its
    own stern code.
In the days to come, though my lips were dumb, in my
    heart how I cursed that load.
In the long, long night, by the lone firelight, while the
    huskies, round in a ring,

Howled out their woes to the homeless snows—O God!
  How I loathed the thing.

And every day that quiet clay seemed to heavy and heavier
  grow;
And on I went, though the dogs were spent and the grub
  was getting low;
The trail was bad, and I felt half mad, but I swore I would
  not give in;
And I'd often sing to the hateful thing, and it hearkened
  with a grin.

Till I came to the marge of Lake Lebarge, and a derelict
  there lay;
It was jammed in the ice, but I saw in a trice it was called
  the 'Alice May'.
And I looked at it, and I thought a bit, and I looked at my
  frozen chum;
Then 'Here,' said I, with a sudden cry, 'is my crematorium.'

Some planks I tore from the cabin floor, and I lit the boiler
  fire;
Some coal I found that was lying around, and I heaped the
  fuel higher;
The flames just soared, and the furnace roared—such a
  blaze you seldom see;
And I burrowed a hole in the glowing coal, and I stuffed in
  Sam McGee.

Then I made a hike, for I didn't like to hear him
  sizzle so;
And the heavens scowled, and the huskies howled, and the
  wind began to blow.

It was icy cold, but the hot sweat rolled down my cheeks,
   and I don't know why;
And the greasy smoke in an inky cloak went streaking
   down the sky.

I do not know how long in the snow I wrestled with grisly
   fear;
But the stars came out and they danced about ere again I
   ventured near;
I was sick with dread, but I bravely said: 'I'll just take a
   peep inside.
I guess he's cooked, and it's time I looked';...then the door
   I opened wide.

And there sat Sam, looking cool and calm, in the heart of
   the furnace roar;
And he wore a smile you could see a mile, and he said:
   'Please close that door.
It's fine in here, but I greatly fear you'll let in the cold and
   storm—
Since I left Plumtree, down in Tennessee, it's the first time
   I've been warm.'

There are strange things done in the midnight sun
   By the men who moil for gold;
The Arctic trails have their secret tales
   That would make your blood run cold;
The Northern Lights have seen queer sights,
   But the queerest they ever did see
Was that night on the marge of Lake Lebarge
   I cremated Sam McGee.

THE HARE AND THE TORTOISE

Vikram Seth

Vikram Seth has a vivid sense of humour that is apparent in his retelling of the well-known fable of the hare and the tortoise. In his version the loser, being a celebrity, is praised, and the winner is ignored. I would love to be back in school, just for the opportunity to recite this superbly written poem. It is a bit long, I agree, but I have left it up to you to edit if you need to. It's a fun piece, so recite it in a light-hearted manner. Keep a lively pace but be careful that you enunciate the words clearly.

Once or twice upon a time
In the land of Runny rhyme
Lived a hare both hot and heady
And a tortoise slow and steady.

When at noon the hare awoke
She would tell herself a joke.
Squeal with laughter, roll about,
Eat her eggs and sauerkraut,
Then pick up the phone and babble,
—'Gibble-gabble, gibble-gabble'—
To her friends the mouse and mole
And the empty-headed vole:
'Hey, girls, did you know the rat
Was rejected by the bat?'
'Good for her! The rat's a fool!'
'Oh, I think he's kinda cool.'
'Too bad, darling, now he's dating
Lady Lemming's maid-in-waiting.'
'What—that hamster? You don't say!'—

Gibble-gabble every day!
Gibble-gabble everywhere
Went the mouse and mole and hare—
Gibble-gabble, gibble-gabble.
Oh, what riffraff! Oh, what rabble!

But the tortoise, when he rose,
Daily counted all his toes
Twice or three times to ensure
There were neither less nor more.
Next he'd tally the amount
In his savings bank account.
Then he'd very carefully
Count his grandsons: one, two, three—
Ed, and Ned, and Fred by name.
And his sermon was the same:
'Eddy, Neddy, Freddy—boys—
You must never break your toys
You must often floss your gums.
You must always do your sums.
Buy your own house; don't pay rent.
Save your funds at six per cent.
Major in accountancy.
And grow up to be like me.
Listen, Eddy, Neddy, Freddy—
You be slow—but you be steady.'

One day by the Fauna Fountain
Near the noble Mammal Mountain
Where the ducks and ducklings dabble,
Hare and mouse went: 'Gibble-gabble,
Gibble-gabble—look who's coming!'

And the hare began a-giggling:
'Well, it isn't Samuel Pigling
—That's for sure—or Peter Rabbit
Or Sir Fox in hunting habit.
Even Hedgehog Roly-Poly
Wouldn't ever walk so slowly.
Inch by inch by inch he's crawling.
How pathetic! How appalling!
He won't get here in an hour
If he uses turtle-power.'

'Teddy Tortoise, go and grab
Tram or train or taxi-cab!'
Squealed the hare; I have no doubt
You can shell the money out!'
And at this disgraceful pun
Hare and mouse both squealed with fun,
Ran around the tortoise twice,
Fell into the fountain thrice,
Swam, and sang out as they swam:
'I'm a tortoise—yes, I am!
See me swimming! Glug, glug, glug!
I'm a tortoise! No, a slug!'

Now the tortoise snapped the air,
And addressed the hare-brained hare:
'Madam, you are rash and young
And should mind your mindless tongue.
Doubtless, Madam, hares exceed
Tortoises by far in speed.
But, were we to run a race,
I, not you, would win first place.

Slowly, surely I'd defeat you.
Trust me, Madam, I would beat you.'

'Darling Tortoise,' drawled the hare,
'I would thrash you anywhere—
Marsh or mountain, hill or dale,
Field or forest, rain or hail!'
Snapped the tortoise slow and steady:
'Choose your place, and I'll be ready.
Choose your time, and make it soon.'
'Here!' the hare said: 'Sunday noon.'

So, at the appointed time
All the beasts of Runny rhyme
—Every reptile, bird, or mammal
From the koala to the camel—
Gathered to behold the race,
Gobbled popcorn, guzzled beer,
And exclaimed: 'They're here! They're here!'
At the starting block the steady
Tortoise flexed his toes, quite ready;
But the flighty hare, still wearing
Her silk nightie, kept on staring
At the mirror while the press
Took her words down, more or less.
Young reporters sought her views
For the 'Rhyme and Runny News'.
'What's at stake besides the honour?'
'Is the tortoise, Ma'am, a goner?'
'Why did you agree to run?'
'Is the race already won?'
Pouting out her scarlet lips,

Sweetly wiggling head and hips,
Making wolves feel weak inside,
Languidly Ms Hare replied:
'Teddy Tortoise, don't you see,
Has this awful crush on me.
Why, he thinks I'm simply stunning.
That's why, darlings, I am running.
And I've staked the cup I won
When I was Miss Honey bun...
Who will win? Why—can't you tell?
Read the lipstick on his shell.'
There she'd smeared a scarlet '2'
And the words: 'Mock Turtil Stew.'

Soon the starting gun was heard
And a secretary bird
Gently murmured: 'It's begun.
Ma'am, perhaps you ought to run.'
'No,' the hare laughed—'Oh, no, no!
Teddy Tortoise is so slow.
Let him have a little start.
I don't want to break his heart.'

But the tortoise plodded on
Like a small automaton,
Muttering, as he held his pace:
'I have got to win this race.'

Two hours passed. In satin shorts
Cut for fashion more than sports,
Ms Hare once again appeared,
Yawning softly as she neared:

'Two o'clock! My beauty sleep!'
'Ma'am, the race—?' 'The race will keep.
Really, it's already won.'
And she stretched out in the sun.

Two hours passed. The hare awoke
And she stretched and yawned and spoke:
'Where's the tortoise?' 'Out of sight.'
'Oh,' the hare said: 'Really? Right!
Time to go—' and off she bounded,
Leaving all her friends astounded
At her rocket-fuelled pace.
'Sure!' they said, 'She'll win this race.'
She was out of sight already
On the heels of Tortoise Teddy.

Suddenly the dizzy hare
Saw a field of mushrooms where
Champignons and chanterelles
Mixed with devils-of-the-dell.
(This last mushroom, I suspect,
Has a cerebral effect.
Every time I eat one, I
Feel I'm floating in the sky.)
'How delicious! What a treat!'
Said the hare: 'I'll stop and eat.'
So she did, and very soon
She was singing out of tune,
And she lurched towards the wood,
Shouting to the neighbourhood:
'Boring, boring, life is boring.
Birdies, help me go exploring.

Let's go off the beaten track.
In a minute I'll be back—'
Off the hare went, fancy-free.
One hour passed, then two, then three.

But the tortoise plodded on
Now the day was almost gone
And the sun was sinking low—
Very steady, very slow—
And he saw the finish line
And he thought, 'The race is mine!'—
And the gold cup was in sight
Glinting in the golden light—
When with an impassioned air
Someone screamed: 'Look! Look! The hare!'—
And the punters started jumping,
And the tortoise heard a thumping
Close behind him on the track,
And he wanted to look back—
For the hare was roused at last
And was gaining on him fast—
And had almost caught him up
And retrieved her golden cup
When the tortoise, mouth agape,
Crossed the line and bit the tape.

After the announcer's gun
Had pronounced that he had won,
And the cheering of the crowd
Died at last, the tortoise bowed,
Clasped the cup with quiet pride,
And sat down, self-satisfied.

And he thought: 'That silly hare!
So much for her charm and flair.
So much for her idle boast.
In her cup I'll raise a toast
To hard work and regularity.
Silly creature! Such vulgarity!
Now she'll learn that sure and slow
Is the only way to go—
That you can't rise to the top
With a skip, a jump, a hop—
That you've got to hatch your eggs,
That you've got to count your legs,
That you've got to do your duty,
Not depend on verve and beauty.
When the press comes, I shall say
That she's been shell-shocked today!
What a well-deserved disgrace
That the fool has lost this race.'

But it was in fact the hare,
With a calm insouciant air
Like an unrepentant bounder,
Who allured the pressmen round her.
'Oh, Miss Hare, you're so appealing
When you're sweating,' said one, squealing.
'You have tendered gold and booty
To the shrine of sleep and beauty,'
Breathed another, overawed;
And Will Wolf, the great press lord
Filled a gold cup—on a whim—
With huge rubies to the brim

—Gorgeous rubies, bold and bright,
Red as cherries, rich with light—
And with an inviting grin
Murmured: 'In my eyes you win.'

And perhaps she had; the hare
Suddenly was everywhere.
Stories of her quotes and capers
Made front page in all the papers—
And the sleepy BBC
—Beastly Broadcast Company—
Beamed a feature in the news:
'All the World Lost for a Snooze'—
Soon she saw her name in lights,
Sold a book and movie rights,
While a travel magazine
Bought the story, sight unseen,
Of her three hour expedition
To the wood—called 'Mushroom Mission'.
Soon the cash came pouring in,
And to save it was a sin—
So she bought a manor house
Where she lived with mole and mouse—
And her friends, when they played Scrabble
Gibble-gabble, gibble-gabble,
Gibble-gabble all the way—
Let her spell Compete with K.

Thus the hare was pampered rotten
And the tortoise was forgotten.

THE TOUCH OF THE MASTER'S HAND

Myra Brooks Welch

Myra Welch suffered from severe arthritis and was confined to a wheelchair. She came from a musical family and herself played the organ till her illness struck. She continued to express the music within her in the form of poetry. She would use the eraser end of a pencil to painstakingly type out each word she wrote. This poem is her masterpiece. If you choose to say this, make sure you watch a video clip of an auction so that you understand how one is conducted.

'Twas battered and scarred, and the auctioneer
Thought it scarcely worth his while
To waste much time on the old violin,
But held it up with a smile.
'What am I bidden, good folks,' he cried,
'Who'll start the bidding for me?'
'A dollar, a dollar'; then 'Two! Only two?
Two dollars, who'll make it three?
Three dollars, once; three dollars, twice;
Going for three—' But no,
From the room, far back, a gray-haired man
Came forward and picked up the bow;
Then, wiping the dust from the old violin,
And tightening the loose strings,
He played a melody pure and sweet
As a caroling angel sings.

The music ceased, and the auctioneer,
With a voice that was quiet and low,
Said: 'What am I bid for the old violin?'
And he held it up with the bow.

'A thousand dollars, and who'll make it two?
Two thousand! And who'll make it three?
Three thousand, once; three thousand, twice,
And going, and going,' said he.
The people cheered, but some of them cried,
We do not quite understand
What changed its worth.' Swift came the reply:
'The touch of a master's hand.'

And many a man with life out of tune,
And battered and scarred with sin,
Is auctioned cheap to the thoughtless crowd,
Much like the old violin.
A 'mess of pottage,' a glass of wine;
A game—and he travels on.
He is 'going once, and 'going' twice,
He's 'going' and almost 'gone.'
But the Master comes, and the foolish crowd
Never can quite understand
The worth of a soul and the change that's wrought
By the touch of the Master's hand.

THE TWO GLASSES

Ella Wheeler Wilcox

This motivational poem compares a glass of plain water to a glass of sparkling wine. The water, despite its simplicity, is the clear winner. The reason why I picked this poem is because it is not very common...and I love the analogy. I suppose students of senior school would do justice to this piece.

There sat two glasses filled to the brim
On a rich man's table, rim to rim,
One was ruddy and red as blood,
And one was clear as the crystal flood.

Said the Glass of Wine to his paler brother:
'Let us tell tales of the past to each other;
I can tell of banquet and revel and mirth,
Where I was king, for I ruled in might;
For the proudest and grandest souls of earth
Fell under my touch, as though struck with blight.
From the heads of kings I have torn the crown;
From the heights of fame I have hurled men down.
I have blasted many an honoured name;
I have taken virtue and given shame;
I have tempted youth with a sip, a taste,
That has made his future a barren waste.
Far greater than any king am I,
Or than any army beneath the sky.
I have made the arm of the driver fail,
And sent the train from the iron rail.
I have made good ships go down at sea.
And the shrieks of the lost were sweet to me.
Fame, strength, wealth, genius before me fall;
And my might and power are over all!
Ho, ho, pale brother,' said the Wine,
'Can you boast of deeds as great as mine?'

Said the Water Glass: 'I cannot boast
Of a king dethroned, or a murdered host;
But I can tell of hearts that were sad,
By my crystal drops made bright and glad;

Of thirsts I have quenched and brows I have laved,
Of hands I have cooled, and souls I have saved.
I have leaped through the valley, dashed down the
    mountain,
Slipped from the sunshine, and dripped from the fountain,
I have burst my cloud-fetters, and dropped from the sky,
And everywhere gladdened the prospect and eye;
I have eased the hot forehead of fever and pain,
I have made the parched meadows grow fertile with grain.
I can tell of the powerful wheel of the mill,
That ground out the flour, and turned at my will.
I can tell of manhood debased by you
That I have uplifted and crowned anew;
I cheer, I help, I strengthen and aid,
I gladden the heart of man and maid;
I set the wine-chained captive free,
And all are better for knowing me.'

These are the tales they told each other,
The Glass of Wine, and its paler brother,
As they sat together, filled to the brim,
On a rich man's table, rim to rim.

THE WRECK ON HIGHWAY 109
Ruth Gillis

*This poem tells a moving story. The emotional quotient is very high in it and there
is a strong rhyme scheme. You can use these to your advantage while conveying the
deep concern of a mother for her children. Your voice should emit the different
emotions, like fear, despair, shock and hope. Start slow as you describe the scene*

A drunk man in an Oldsmobile they said had run the
    light
That caused the six-car pileup on 109 that night.
When broken bodies lay about and blood was everywhere,
The sirens screamed out elegies, for death was in the air.

A mother, trapped inside her car, was heard above the
    noise;
Her plaintive plea near split the air 'Oh, God, please spare
    my boys!'
She fought to loose her pinioned hands; she struggled to
    get free,
But mangled metal held her fast in grim captivity.

Her frightened eyes then focused on where the backseat
    once had been,
But all she saw was broken glass and two children's seats
    crushed in.
Her twins were nowhere to be seen; she did not hear them
    cry,
And then she prayed they'd been thrown free, 'Oh, God,
    don't let them die!'

Then firemen came and cut her loose, but when they
    searched the back,
They found therein no little boys, but the seat belts were
    intact.
They thought the woman had gone mad and was traveling
    alone,

But when they turned to question her, they discovered she
    was gone.

Policemen saw her running wild and screaming above the
    noise
In beseeching supplication, 'Please help me find my boys!
They're four years old and wear blue shirts; their jeans are
    blue to match.'
One cop spoke up, 'They're in my car, and they don't have
    a scratch.

'They said their daddy put them there and gave them each
    a cone,
Then told them both to wait for Mom to come and take
    them home.
I've searched the area high and low, but I can't find their
    dad.
He must have fled the scene, I guess, and that is very bad.'

The mother hugged the twins and said, while wiping at a
    tear,
'He could not flee the scene, you see, for he's been dead a
    year.
The cop just looked confused and asked, 'Now, how can
    that be true?'
The boys said, 'Mommy, Daddy came and left a kiss for
    you.

'He told us not to worry and that you would be all right,
And then he put us in this car with the pretty, flashing
    light.
We wanted him to stay with us, because we miss him so,
But Mommy, he just hugged us tight and said he had to go.

'He said someday we'd understand and told us not to fuss,
And he said to tell you, Mommy, he's watching over us.'
The mother knew without a doubt that what they spoke
     was true,
For she recalled their dad's last words, 'I will watch over
     you.'

The firemen's notes could not explain the twisted, mangled
     car,
And how the three of them escaped without a single scar.
But on the cop's report was scribed, in print so very fine,
An angel walked the beat tonight on Highway 109.

THE YOUNG MAN WAITED

Edmund Vance Cooke

*This one is about a young suitor waiting for his lady to appear. She is upstairs
getting ready and obviously taking her time about it. An interesting poem, it is
ideal for a boy. It is a fun piece and the punch is in the last line of each stanza. As
you proceed through the poem, each successive 'last line' should emote the gradual
increase in the impatience felt by the suitor, by emphasizing on the different words
that describe 'how he waited'.*

In the room below the young man sat,
With an anxious face and a white cravat,
A throbbing heart and a silken hat,
And various other things like that
Which he had accumulated.
And the maid of his heart was up above
Surrounded by hat and gown and glove,

And a thousand things which women love,
But no man knoweth the names thereof—
And the young man sat and—waited.

You will scarce believe the things I tell,
But the truth thereof I know full well,
Though how may not be stated;
But I swear to you that the maiden took
A sort of half-breed, thin stove-hook,
And heated it well in the gaslight there.
And thrust it into her head, or hair.
Then she took something off the bed,
And hooked it onto her hair, or head,
And piled it high, and piled it higher,
And drove it home with staples of wire!
And the young man anxiously—waited.

Then she took a thing she called a 'puff'
And some very peculiar whitish stuff,
And using about a half a peck,
She spread it over her face and neck,
(Deceit was a thing she hated!)
And she looked as fair as a lilied bower,
Or a pound of lard or a sack of flour;—
And the young man wearily—waited.

Then she took a garment of awful shape
And it wasn't a waist, nor yet a cape,
But it looked like a piece of ancient mail,
Or an instrument from a Russian jail,
And then with a fearful groan and gasp,
She squeezed herself in its deathly clasp—

So fair and yet so fated!
And then with a move like I don't know what,
She tied it on with a double knot;—
And the young man woefully—waited.

Then she put on a dozen different things,
A mixture of buttons and hooks and strings,
Till she strongly resembled a notion store;
Then, taking some seventeen pins or more,
She thrust them into her ruby lips,
Then stuck them around from waist to hips,
And never once hesitated.
And the maiden didn't know, perhaps,
That the man below had had seven naps,
And that now he sleepily—waited.

And then she tried to put on her hat,
Ah me, a trying ordeal was that!
She tipped it high and she tried it low,
But every way that the thing would go
Only made her more agitated.
It wouldn't go straight and it caught her hair,
And she wished she could hire a man to swear,
But alas, the only man lingering there
Was the one who wildly—waited.

And then before she could take her leave,
She had to puff up her monstrous sleeve.
Then a little dab here and a wee pat there.
And a touch or two to her hindmost hair,
Then around the room with the utmost care
She thoughtfully circulated.

Then she seized her gloves and a chamoiskin,
Some breath perfume and a long stickpin,
A bonbon box and a cloak and some
Eau-de-cologne and chewing-gum,
Her opera glass and sealskin muff,
A fan and a heap of other stuff;
Then she hurried down, but ere she spoke,
Something about the maiden broke.
So she scurried back to the winding stair,
And the young man looked in wild despair,
And then he—evaporated.

Prose and Drama

THE EMPEROR'S NEW CLOTHES

Hans Christian Andersen

Hans Christian Andersen was a brilliant storyteller. This is one of his classics about a vain and materialistic emperor. Become the storyteller. Keep your voice soft and light and exhibit the wit and humour of the piece.

Many years ago there was an Emperor so exceedingly fond of new clothes that he spent all his money on being well dressed. He cared nothing about reviewing his soldiers, going to the theatre, or going for a ride in his carriage, except to show off his new clothes.

In the great city where he lived, life was always gay. Every day many strangers came to town, and among them one day came two swindlers. They let it be known they were weavers, and they said they could weave the most magnificent fabrics imaginable. Not only were their colours and patterns uncommonly fine, but clothes made of this cloth had a wonderful way of becoming invisible to anyone who was unfit for his office, or who was unusually stupid.

'Those would be just the clothes for me,' thought the Emperor. 'If I wore them I would be able to discover which men in my empire are unfit for their posts. And I could tell the wise men from the fools.' He paid the two swindlers a large sum of money to start work at once.

They set up two looms and pretended to weave, though there was nothing on the looms. All the finest silk and the purest old thread which they demanded went into their travelling bags, while they worked the empty looms far into the night.

'I'd like to know how those weavers are getting on with the cloth,' the Emperor thought, but he felt slightly uncomfortable when he remembered that those who were unfit for their position would not be able to see the fabric.

'I'll send my honest old minister to the weavers,' the Emperor decided. 'He'll be the best one to tell me how the material looks, for he's a sensible man and no one does his duty better.'

So the honest old minister went to the room where the two swindlers sat working away at their empty looms.

'Heaven help me,' he thought as his eyes flew wide open, 'I can't see anything at all'. But he did not say so.

Both the swindlers begged him to be so kind as to come near to approve the excellent pattern, the beautiful colours. They pointed to the empty looms, and the poor old minister stared as hard as he dared. He couldn't see anything, because there was nothing to see. 'Heaven have mercy,' he thought. 'Can it be that I'm a fool? I'd have never guessed it, and not a soul must know. Am I unfit to be the minister? It would never do to let on that I can't see the cloth.'

'Don't hesitate to tell us what you think of it,' said one of the weavers.

'Oh, it's beautiful—it's enchanting.' The old minister peered through his spectacles. 'Such a pattern, what colours! I'll be sure to tell the Emperor how delighted I am with it.'

'We're pleased to hear that,' the swindlers said. They proceeded to name all the colours and to explain the intricate pattern. The old minister paid the closest attention, so that he could tell it all to the Emperor. And so he did.

The swindlers at once asked for more money, more silk and gold thread, to get on with the weaving. But it all went into their pockets. Not a thread went into the looms, though they worked at their weaving as hard as ever.

The Emperor presently sent another trustworthy official to see how the work progressed and how soon it would be ready. The same thing happened to him that had happened to the minister. He looked and he looked, but as there was nothing to see in the looms he couldn't see anything.

'Isn't it a beautiful piece of goods?' the swindlers asked him, as they displayed and described their imaginary pattern.

'I know I'm not stupid,' the man thought, 'so it must be that I'm unworthy of my good office. That's strange. I mustn't let anyone find it out, though.' So he praised the material he did not see. He declared he was delighted with the beautiful colours and the exquisite pattern. To the Emperor he said, 'It held me spellbound.'

All the town was talking of this splendid cloth, and the Emperor wanted to see it for himself while it was still in the looms. Attended by a band of chosen men, among whom were his two old trusted officials—the ones who had been to the weavers—he set out to see the two swindlers. He found them weaving with might and main, but without a thread in their looms.

'Magnificent,' said the two officials already duped. 'Just look, Your Majesty, what colours! What a design!' They pointed to the empty looms, each supposing that the others could see the stuff.

'What's this?' thought the Emperor. 'I can't see anything. This is terrible!

Am I a fool? Am I unfit to be the Emperor? What a thing to happen to me of all people!—'Oh! It's very pretty,' he said. 'It has my highest approval.' And he nodded approbation at the empty loom. Nothing could make him say that he couldn't see anything.

His whole retinue stared and stared. One saw no more than another, but they all joined the Emperor in exclaiming, 'Oh! It's very pretty,' and they advised him to wear clothes made of this wonderful cloth especially for the great procession he was soon to lead. 'Magnificent! Excellent! Unsurpassed!' were bandied from mouth to mouth, and everyone did his best to seem well pleased. The Emperor gave each of the swindlers a cross to wear in his buttonhole, and the title of 'Sir Weaver.'

Before the procession the swindlers sat up all night and burned more than six candles, to show how busy they were finishing the Emperor's new clothes. They pretended to take the cloth off the loom. They made cuts in the air with huge scissors. And at last they said, 'Now the Emperor's new clothes are ready for him.'

Then the Emperor himself came with his noblest noblemen, and the swindlers each raised an arm as if they were holding something. They said, 'These are the trousers, here's the coat, and this is the mantle,' naming each garment. 'All of them are as light as a spider web. One would almost think he had nothing on, but that's what makes them so fine.'

'Exactly,' all the noblemen agreed, though they could see nothing, for there was nothing to see.

'If Your Imperial Majesty will condescend to take your clothes off,' said the swindlers, 'we will help you on with your new ones here in front of the long mirror.'

The Emperor undressed, and the swindlers pretended to put his new clothes on him, one garment after another.

'How well Your Majesty's new clothes look. Aren't they becoming!' He heard on all sides, 'That pattern, so perfect! Those colours, so suitable! It is a magnificent outfit.'

Then the minister of public processions announced: 'Your

Majesty's canopy is waiting outside.'

So off went the Emperor in procession under his splendid canopy. Everyone in the streets and the windows said, 'Oh, how fine are the Emperor's new clothes! Don't they fit him to perfection? And see his long train!' Nobody would confess that he couldn't see anything, for that would prove him either unfit for his position, or a fool.

'But he hasn't got anything on,' a little child said.

'Did you ever hear such innocent prattle?' said its father. And one person whispered to another what the child had said, 'He hasn't anything on. A child says he hasn't anything on.'

'But he hasn't got anything on!' the whole town cried out at last.

The Emperor shivered, for he suspected they were right. But he thought, 'This procession has got to go on.' So he walked more proudly than ever, as his noblemen held high the train that wasn't there at all.

TO BE, OR NOT TO BE

Hamlet's soliloquy from Hamlet
William Shakespeare

This is arguably Shakespeare's most recognizable soliloquy. The underlying theme here is Hamlet's inaction and his frustration at his own weaknesses. The biggest negative that I can see in this piece is that it is too well known. But it is still a classic and ideal for class elocution.

To be, or not to be—that is the question:
Whether 'tis nobler in the mind to suffer
The slings and arrows of outrageous fortune

Or to take arms against a sea of troubles
And by opposing end them. To die, to sleep—
No more—and by a sleep to say we end
The heartache, and the thousand natural shocks
That flesh is heir to. 'Tis a consummation
Devoutly to be wished. To die, to sleep—
To sleep—perchance to dream: ay, there's the rub,
For in that sleep of death what dreams may come
When we have shuffled off this mortal coil,
Must give us pause. There's the respect
That makes calamity of so long life.
For who would bear the whips and scorns of time,
Th' oppressor's wrong, the proud man's contumely
The pangs of despised love, the law's delay,
The insolence of office, and the spurns
That patient merit of th' unworthy takes,
When he himself might his quietus make
With a bare bodkin? Who would fardels bear,
To grunt and sweat under a weary life,
But that the dread of something after death,
The undiscovered country, from whose bourn
No traveller returns, puzzles the will,
And makes us rather bear those ills we have
Than fly to others that we know not of?
Thus conscience does make cowards of us all,
And thus the native hue of resolution
Is sicklied o'er with the pale cast of thought,
And enterprise of great pitch and moment
With this regard their currents turn awry
And lose the name of action.—Soft you now,
The fair Ophelia!—Nymph, in thy orisons
Be all my sins remembered.

From UNCLE PODGER HANGS A PICTURE

Jerome K. Jerome

'Little knowledge is a dangerous thing,' says the proverb. Even the simplest of tasks may seem difficult in the hands of an amateur. This hilarious piece is an extract from Jerome K. Jerome's classic Three Men in a Boat. *What makes it all the more laughable is that many of us have an 'Uncle Podger' in our family.*

You never saw such a commotion up and down a house, in all your life, as when my Uncle Podger undertook to do a job. A picture would have come home from the frame-maker's, and be standing in the dining-room, waiting to be put up; and Aunt Podger would ask what was to be done with it, and Uncle Podger would say:

'Oh, you leave that to me. Don't you, any of you, worry yourselves about that. I'll do all that.'

And then he would take off his coat, and begin. He would send the girl out for sixpen'orth of nails, and then one of the boys after her to tell her what size to get; and, from that, he would gradually work down, and start the whole house.

'Now you go and get me my hammer, Will,' he would shout; 'and you bring me the rule, Tom; and I shall want the step-ladder, and I had better have a kitchen-chair, too; and, Jim! you run round to Mr Goggles, and tell him, 'Pa's kind regards, and hopes his leg's better; and will he lend him his spirit-level?' And don't you go, Maria, because I shall want somebody to hold me the light; and when the girl comes back, she must go out again for a bit of picture-cord; and Tom!—where's Tom?—Tom, you come here; I shall want you to hand me up the picture.'

And then he would lift up the picture, and drop it, and

it would come out of the frame, and he would try to save the glass, and cut himself; and then he would spring round the room, looking for his handkerchief. He could not find his handkerchief, because it was in the pocket of the coat he had taken off, and he did not know where he had put the coat, and all the house had to leave off looking for his tools, and start looking for his coat; while he would dance round and hinder them.

'Doesn't anybody in the whole house know where my coat is? I never came across such a set in all my life—upon my word I didn't. Six of you!—and you can't find a coat that I put down not five minutes ago! Well, of all the—'

Then he'd get up, and find that he had been sitting on it, and would call out:

'Oh, you can give it up! I've found it myself now. Might just as well ask the cat to find anything as expect you people to find it.'

And, when half an hour had been spent in tying up his finger, and a new glass had been got, and the tools, and the ladder, and the chair, and the candle had been brought, he would have another go, the whole family, including the girl and the charwoman, standing round in a semicircle, ready to help. Two people would have to hold the chair, and a third would help him up on it, and hold him there, and a fourth would hand him a nail, and a fifth would pass him up the hammer, and he would take hold of the nail, and drop it.

'There!' he would say, in an injured tone, 'now the nail's gone.'

And we would all have to go down on our knees and grovel for it, while he would stand on the chair, and grunt, and want to know if he was to be kept there all the evening.

The nail would be found at last, but by that time he would have lost the hammer.

'Where's the hammer? What did I do with the hammer? Great heavens! Seven of you, gaping round there, and you don't know what I did with the hammer!'

We would find the hammer for him, and then he would have lost sight of the mark he had made on the wall, where the nail was to go in, and each of us had to get up on the chair, beside him, and see if we could find it; and we would each discover it in a different place, and he would call us all fools, one after another, and tell us to get down. And he would take the rule, and remeasure, and find that he wanted half thirty-one and three-eighths inches from the corner, and would try to do it in his head, and go mad.

And we would all try to do it in our heads, and all arrive at different results, and sneer at one another. And in the general row, the original number would be forgotten, and Uncle Podger would have to measure it again.

He would use a bit of string this time, and at the critical moment, when the old fool was leaning over the chair at an angle of forty-five, and trying to reach a point three inches beyond what was possible for him to reach, the string would slip, and down he would slide on to the piano, a really fine musical effect being produced by the suddenness with which his head and body struck all the notes at the same time.

And Aunt Maria would say that she would not allow the children to stand round and hear such language.

At last, Uncle Podger would get the spot fixed again, and put the point of the nail on it with his left hand, and take the hammer in his right hand. And, with the first blow, he would smash his thumb, and drop the hammer, with a yell, on somebody's toes.

Aunt Maria would mildly observe that, next time Uncle Podger was going to hammer a nail into the wall, she hoped he'd let her know in time, so that she could make arrangements to go and spend a week with her mother while it was being done.

'Oh! you women, you make such a fuss over everything,' Uncle Podger would reply, picking himself up. 'Why, I like doing a little job of this sort.'

And then he would have another try, and, at the second blow, the nail would go clean through the plaster, and half the hammer after it, and Uncle Podger be precipitated against the wall with force nearly sufficient to flatten his nose.

Then we had to find the rule and the string again, and a new hole was made; and, about midnight, the picture would be up—very crooked and insecure, the wall for yards round looking as if it had been smoothed down with a rake, and everybody dead beat and wretched—except Uncle Podger.

'There you are,' he would say, stepping heavily off the chair on to the charwoman's corns, and surveying the mess he had made with evident pride. 'Why, some people would have had a man in to do a little thing like that!'

WHY CAN'T THE ENGLISH
From My Fair Lady

Here is a delightful piece that is sure to entertain! Perhaps it would be helpful if one were to watch the piece on video and then make an attempt to recite it. It's a truly memorable piece from the multiple Oscar-winning film. And let me tell you a secret: this was my favourite piece in school and I have won a number of first prizes reciting it!

Harrison: Look at her, a victim of the gutters,
Condemned by every syllable she utters.
By right she should be taken out and hung,
For the cold-blooded murder of the English tongue.

(Meow!) Heavens, what a sound!
This is what the English population,
Calls an elementary education.

Bystander: Come sir, I think you've picked a poor
example.

Harrison: Did I?
Hear them down in Soho Square,
Dropping 'H's' everywhere,
Speaking English any way they like.
You sir, did you go to school?

Bystander: Whatta tyke me for, a fool?

Harrison: No one taught him 'take' instead of 'tyke'.
Hear a Yorkshireman, or worse,
Hear a Cornishman converse.
I'd rather hear a choir singing flat.
Just like this one.
(Garn!)
I ask you sir, what sort of word is that?

It's Au and Garn that keep her in her place
Not her wretched clothes and dirty face.
Why can't the English teach their children how to speak.
This verbal class distinction by now should be antique.
If you spoke sir, instead of the way you do,
Why you might be selling flowers too.

Bystander: I beg your pardon.

Harrison: An Englishman's way of speaking absolutely
    classifies him.
The moment he talks he makes some other Englishman
    despise him.
One common language I'm afraid we'll never get.
Oh why can't the English, learn to set a good example
 To people whose English is painful to your ears?
The Scotch and the Irish leave you close to tears.
There are even places where English completely disappears.
Well, in America they haven't used it for years.

Why can't the English teach their children how to speak?
Norwegians learn Norwegian, the Greeks are taught their
    Greek.
In France every Frenchman knows his language from A to
    Zed.
The French don't care what they do, actually,
As long as they pronounce it properly.
Arabians learn Arabian with the speed of summer lightning,
And Hebrews learn it backward which is absolutely
    frightening.

If you use proper English you're regarded as a freak.
Oh why can't the English,
Why can't the English
Learn to speak!

THE KITEMAKER

Ruskin Bond

Mahmood the kitemaker's business is suffering because the younger generation would rather watch films than fly kites. He is now a poor person. He makes kites for his grandson Ali. One day, while he sits thinking of his grand old days and watches Ali fly kites, he loses consciousness. A classic piece by our country's ace storyteller.

There was but one tree in the street known as Gali Ram Nathan. An ancient banyan that had grown through the cracks of an abandoned mosque—and little Ali's kite had caught in its branches. The boy, barefoot and clad only in a torn shirt, ran along the cobbled stones of the narrow street to where his grandfather sat nodding dreamily in the sunshine of their back courtyard.

'Grandfather,' shouted the boy. 'My kite has gone!'

The old man woke from his daydream with a start and, raising his head, displayed a beard that would have been white had it not been dyed red with mehendi leaves.

'Did the twine break?' he asked. 'I know that kite twine is not what it used to be.'

'No, Grandfather, the kite is stuck in the banyan tree.'

The old man chuckled. 'You have yet to learn how to fly a kite properly, my child. And I am too old to teach you, that's the pity of it. But you shall have another.'

He had just finished making a new kite from bamboo paper and thin silk, and it lay in the sun, firming up. It was a pale, pink kite, with a small, green tail. The old man handed it to Ali, and the boy raised himself on his toes and kissed his grandfather's hollowed-out cheek.

'I will not lose this one,' he said. 'This kite will fly like a bird.' And he turned on his heels and skipped out of the courtyard.

The old man remained dreaming in the sun. His kite shop was gone, the premises long since sold to a junk dealer; but he still made kites, for his own amusement and for the benefit of his grandson, Ali. Not many people bought kites these days. Adults disdained them, and children preferred to spend their money at the cinema. Moreover, there were not many open spaces left for the flying of kites. The city had swallowed up the open grassland that had stretched from the old fort's walls to the river bank.

But the old man remembered a time when grown men flew kites, and great battles were fought, the kites swerving and swooping in the sky, tangling with each other until the string of one was severed. Then the defeated but liberated kite would float away into the blue unknown. There was a good deal of betting, and money frequently changed hands.

Kite-flying was then the sport of kings, and the old man remembered how the Nawab himself would come down to the riverside with his retinue to participate in this noble pastime. There was time, then, to spend an idle hour with a gay, dancing strip of paper. Now everyone hurried, in a heat of hope, and delicate things like kites and daydreams were trampled underfoot.

He, Mehmood the kitemaker, had in the prime of his life been well known throughout the city. Some of his more elaborate kites once sold for as much as three or four rupees each.

At the request of the Nawab he had once made a very special kind of kite, unlike any that had been seen in the district. It consisted of a series of small, very light paper disks trailing on a thin bamboo frame.

Everyone had heard of the 'Dragon Kite' that Mehmood had built, and word went round that it possessed supernatural powers. A large crowd assembled in the open to watch its first public launching in the presence of the Nawab.

At the first attempt it refused to leave the ground. The disks made a plaintive, protesting sound, and the sun was trapped in the little mirrors, making of the kite a living, complaining creature. Then the wind came from the right direction, and the Dragon Kite soared into the sky, wriggling its way higher and higher, the sun still glinting in its devil-eyes. And when it went very high, it pulled fiercely on the twine, and Mehmood's young sons had to help him with the reel. Still the kite pulled, determined to be free, to break loose, to live a life of its own. And eventually it did so.

The twine snapped, the kite leaped away towards the sun, sailing on heavenward until it was lost to view. It was never found again, and Mehmood wondered afterwards if he made too vivid, too living a thing of the great kite. He did not make another like it. Instead he presented to the Nawab a musical kite, one that made a sound like a violin when it rose in the air.

Those were more leisurely, more spacious days. But the Nawab had died years ago, and his descendants were almost as poor as Mehmood himself. Kitemakers, like poets, once had their patrons; but no one knew Mehmood, simply because there were too many people in the Gali, and they could not be bothered with their neighbours.

When Mehmood was younger and had fallen sick, everyone in the neighbourhood had come to ask after his health; but now, when his days were drawing to a close, no one visited him. Most of his old friends were dead and his sons had grown up: one was working in a local garage and the other, who was in Pakistan at the time of the Partition, had not been able to rejoin his relatives.

The children who had bought kites from him ten years ago were now grown men, struggling for a living; they did not have time for the old man and his memories. They had grown up in a swiftly changing and competitive world, and they looked at the old kitemaker and the banyan tree with the same indifference.

No longer did people gather under the banyan tree to discuss their problems and their plans; only in the summer months did a few seek shelter from the fierce sun.

But there was the boy, his grandson. It was good that Mehmood's son worked close by, for it gladdened the old man's heart to watch the small boy at play in the winter sunshine, growing under his eyes like a young and well-nourished sapling putting forth new leaves each day.

Mehmood was like the banyan, his hands gnarled and twisted like the roots of the ancient tree. Ali was like the young mimosa planted at the end of the courtyard. In two years both he and the tree would acquire the strength and confidence of their early youth.

The voices in the street grew fainter, and Mehmood wondered if he was going to fall asleep and dream, as he so often did, of a kite so beautiful and powerful that it would resemble the great white bird of the Hindus—Garuda, God Vishnu's famous steed. He would like to make a wonderful new kite for little Ali. He had nothing else to leave the boy.

He heard Ali's voice in the distance, but did not realize that the boy was calling him. The voice seemed to come from very far away.

Ali was at the courtyard door, asking if his mother had as yet returned from the bazaar. When Mehmood did not answer, the boy came forward repeating his question. The sunlight was slanting across the old man's head, and a small white butterfly rested on his flowing beard. Mehmood was silent; and when Ali put his small brown hand on the old man's shoulder, he met with no response. The boy heard a faint sound, like the rubbing of marbles in his pocket.

Suddenly afraid, Ali turned and moved to the door, and then ran down the street shouting for his mother. The butterfly left the old man's beard and flew to the mimosa tree, and a sudden gust of wind caught the torn kite and lifted it in the air, carrying it far above the struggling city into the blind blue sky.

FRIENDS, ROMANS, COUNTRYMEN

Mark Antony's speech from Julius Caesar
William Shakespeare

This is Mark Antony's famous speech on the death of Caesar. Remember, in the play, his oration followed that of Brutus's, and it was this speech that touched the very souls of his countrymen, and ignited in them the fire to oppose Brutus's claims. Though it is a common choice for elocution, it remains a classic, simply because of the stirring passion with which it needs to be said.

Friends, Romans, countrymen, lend me your ears;
I come to bury Caesar, not to praise him;
The evil that men do lives after them,
The good is oft interred with their bones,
So let it be with Caesar... The noble Brutus
Hath told you Caesar was ambitious:

If it were so, it was a grievous fault,
And grievously hath Caesar answered it...
Here, under leave of Brutus and the rest,
(For Brutus is an honourable man;
So are they all; all honourable men)
Come I to speak in Caesar's funeral...
He was my friend, faithful and just to me:
But Brutus says he was ambitious;
And Brutus is an honourable man...
He hath brought many captives home to Rome,
Whose ransoms did the general coffers fill:
Did this in Caesar seem ambitious?
When that the poor have cried, Caesar hath wept:
Ambition should be made of sterner stuff:
Yet Brutus says he was ambitious;
And Brutus is an honourable man.
You all did see that on the Lupercal
I thrice presented him a kingly crown,
Which he did thrice refuse: was this ambition?
Yet Brutus says he was ambitious;
And, sure, he is an honourable man.
I speak not to disprove what Brutus spoke,
But here I am to speak what I do know.
You all did love him once, not without cause:
What cause withholds you then to mourn for him?
O judgement! Thou art fled to brutish beasts,
And men have lost their reason... Bear with me;
My heart is in the coffin there with Caesar,
And I must pause till it come back to me.

I'M AN ORDINARY MAN
From My Fair Lady

My Fair Lady is a perennially popular film. It was released in 1964 and won seven Academy awards. This piece is Henry Higgins' early song, confirming he is a 'quiet living man' without the need for a woman. There must be a lot of conviction in your voice as you recite this. Please ensure that you do not sing it the way Higgins did—he was singing...you are reciting.

Well after all, Pickering, I'm an ordinary man,
Who desires nothing more than an ordinary chance,
to live exactly as he likes, and do precisely what he wants...
An average man am I, of no eccentric whim,
Who likes to live his life, free of strife,
Doing whatever he thinks is best, for him,
Well...just an ordinary man...
BUT, Let a woman in your life and your serenity is
    through,
She'll redecorate your home, from the cellar to the dome,
and then go on to the enthralling fun of overhauling you...
Let a woman in your life, and you're up against a wall,
Make a plan and you will find,
That she has something else in mind,
And so rather than do either you do something else
That neither likes at all. You want to talk of Keats and Milton,
She only wants to talk of love,
You go to see a play or ballet, and spend it searching
For her glove, let a woman in your life
And you invite eternal strife,
Let them buy their wedding bands for those anxious little
    hands...

I'd be equally as willing for a dentist to be drilling
Than to ever let a woman in my life. I'm a very gentle man,
Even tempered and good natured
Who you never hear complain,
Who has the milk of human kindness
By the quart in every vein,
A patient man am I, down to my fingertips,
The sort who never could, ever would,
Let an insulting remark escape his lips
Very gentle man...
But, let a woman in your life,
And patience hasn't got a chance,
She will beg you for advice, your reply will be concise,
And she will listen very nicely, and then go out
And do exactly what she wants!!!
You are a man of grace and polish,
Who never spoke above a hush,
All at once you're using language that would make
A sailor blush, Let a woman in your life,
And you're plunging in a knife,
Let the others of my sex, tie the knot around their necks,
I prefer a new edition of the Spanish Inquisition
Than to ever let a woman in my life I'm a quiet living man,
Who prefers to spend the evening in the silence of his
    room,
Who likes an atmosphere as restful as an undiscovered
    tomb,
A pensive man am I, of philosophical joys,
Who likes to meditate, contemplate,
Far for humanities mad inhuman noise,
Quiet living man...

But, let a woman in your life, and your sabbatical is
    through,
In a line that never ends comes an army of her friends,
Come to jabber and to chatter
And to tell her what the matter is with YOU!,
She'll have a booming boisterous family,
Who will descend on you en mass,
She'll have a large wagnarian mother,
With a voice that shatters glass,
Let a woman in your life,
Let a woman in your life,
Let a woman in your life I shall never let a woman in my
    life.

MIDDLE & SENIOR SCHOOL

From THE SON OF MAN
Dennis Potter

Dennis Potter was an English television dramatist, screenwriter and journalist. Here is Dennis Potter at his best—an excerpt from his critically acclaimed play of the same name. A supremely powerful piece, if said with the right expression and feeling, is a sure winner. Extremely moving, in the hands of a gifted elocutionist it could move one to tears.

You have come together here in this place
You have things in common, O cosy, cosy, people
You are safe here.
The world may be falling apart
Soldiers may be waiting...heads are breaking
But not here...not now...
It's alright here, calm here, safe here, cosy here.
So go on—touch each other.
You there you too; go on—touch.
Go on, don't be frightened;
Hold each other by the hand.
It's nice...very nice?
But it's easy eh, easy?
It's easy to love your brother
Easy to love those who are like you?
Why even the tax collectors can do that!

But what tell me then, dear safe, cosy, smug people?
What is so extraordinary about holding the hand of your
    own brothers and sisters, Hmmm?
Do you want me to congratulate you for loving those who
    love you?

Love your enemies, love your enemies
This is what I have come to tell you: Love your enemies.
Love the man who hates you, love the man who kicks and
    spits on you,
Love the brigand who robs and tortures you
Love the soldier who drives his sword into your belly...
Love your enemies.

Set your minds on this
On God's justice and on God's kingdom.
Never mind about money.
You cannot love money and love God,
You cannot love money and love your fellowman,
And your fellowman is God.
Where else is God? Think of what that means.
Think of all the wars and sufferings
And starvations and exploitations.
When are you going to stop it?
When are you going to change it?
When are YOU going to change?

Begin here, begin now!
Open your minds...
See the world as it might be...as it could be.

Ask and you will receive
Seek and you will find
Knock and the door will be opened!

Now? Yes this very moment!
But only if you begin now, with love.
Not easy love—
Not simple love—

But the hard kind.
The kind that topples the giants, that blunts the sword
That empties the prisons and makes money useless.
The hardest love of all—the love that hurts…
The love for your enemies!
This is what I have come to tell you
Will you listen, oh will you listen to me?

I DEMAND DEATH

Fulton J. Sheen

Fulton J. Sheen was a charismatic archbishop who is considered to be one of the first televangelists, having won two Emmies for his show in which he preached about morals and living a good life. This powerful piece is credited to Fulton, and is extremely popular and readily available on the Internet. It is an actor's dream; it demands depth, passion, intensity, drama, pity and an entire spectrum of emotions.

My hands are wet with blood. They are crimsoned with the blood of a man I have just killed.

I have come here today to confess. I have committed murder, deliberate, premeditated murder. I have killed a man in cold blood. That man is my master.

I am here not to ask for pity but for justice. Simple, elementary justice. I am a tenant… My father was a tenant before me and so was his father before him. This misery is my inheritance and perhaps this will be my legacy to my children.

I have laboured on a patch of land not mine. But I have learned to love that land, for it is the only thing that lies between me and complete destitution.

It is the only world that I have learned to cherish. And somewhere on that land I have managed to build what is now the dilapidated nipa shack that has been home to me.

I have but a few world possessions, mostly rags. My debts are heavy. They are the sum total of my ignorance and the inspired arithmetic of my master, which I do not understand.

I labour like a slave and out of the fruits of that labour I get but a mere pittance for a share. And I have to stretch that mere pittance to keep myself and my family alive.

My poverty has reduced me to the bare necessities of life. And the constant fear of rejection from the land has made me totally subservient to my master. You tell me that under the constitution, I am a free man—free to do what I believe is just, free to do what I think is right, and free to worship God according to the dictate of my conscience. But I do not understand the meaning of all these for I have never known freedom. I have always obeyed the wishes of my master out of fear. I have always regarded myself as no better than a slave to the man who owns the land on which I live. I do not ask you to forgive me nor to mitigate my crime. I have taken the law into my own hands, and I must pay for it in atonement.

But kill this system. Kill this system and you kill despotism. Kill this system and you kill slavery. Kill this despotism and you set the human soul to liberty and freedom. Kill this slavery and you release the human spirit into happiness and contentment. For the cause of human liberty, of human happiness and contentment, thousands and even millions have died and will continue to die.

Mine is only one life. Take me if you must but let it be a sacrifice to the cause which countless others have been given before and will be given again and again, until the oppressive economic system has completely perished, until the sons of toil have been liberated from enslavement, and until man has been fully restored to decency and self-respect.

You tell me of the right to life and liberty and the pursuit of happiness. But I have known no rights, only obligations; I have known no happiness; only despair in the encumbered existence that has always been my lot.

My dear friend, I am a peace-loving citizen. I have nothing but love for my fellowmen. And yet, why did I kill this man? It is because he was the symbol of an economic system which has made him and me what we are: he, a master, and I, a slave.

Out of a deliberate design I killed him because I could no longer stand this life of constant fear and being a servant. I could no longer suffer the thought of being perpetually a slave.

I committed the murder as an abject lesson. I want the blow that spelled the death of my master to be a death blow to the institution of the economic slavery which shamelessly exists in the bright sunlight of freedom that is guaranteed by the constitution to every man. In pursuance of the same retribution of justice, to an economic system that has brought an insistent but bootless cry of anguish from the weak and helpless and has laid upon the back of the ignorant labour burdens that are too heavy to be borne, I demand death!

To this callous system of exploitation that has tightened the fetters of perpetual bondage in the hands of thousands, and has killed the spirit of freedom in the hearts of men, I demand death.

To this oppression that has denied liberty to the free and unbounded children of God, I DEMAND DEATH!

IS THIS A DAGGER WHICH I SEE BEFORE ME

Macbeth's soliloquy from Macbeth
William Shakespeare

Shakespeare has given us so many wonderful pieces which are sure winners at any elocution contest. This is one of his best. Picture this: it is totally silent and pitch-black. It is now or never. Macbeth stares into the darkness. He sees a dagger hanging in mid-air before him. He closes his eyes and opens them again. It is still there. It doesn't waver. Is it really a dagger? Put yourself in Macbeth's shoes...become him.

Is this a dagger which I see before me,
The handle toward my hand? Come, let me clutch thee!
I have thee not, and yet I see thee still.
Art thou not, fatal vision, sensible
To feeling as to sight? or art thou but
A dagger of the mind, a false creation
Proceeding from the heat-oppressèd brain?
I see thee yet, in form as palpable
As this which now I draw.
Thou marshall'st me the way that I was going,
And such an instrument I was to use.
Mine eyes are made the fools o' th' other senses,
Or else worth all the rest. I see thee still,
And on thy blade and dudgeon gouts of blood,
Which was not so before. There's no such thing.
It is the bloody business which informs
Thus to mine eyes. Now o'er the one half-world
Nature seems dead, and wicked dreams abuse
The curtained sleep. Witchcraft celebrates
Pale Hecate's offerings; and withered murder,

Alarumed by his sentinel, the wolf,
Whose howl's his watch, thus with his stealthy pace,
With Tarquin's ravishing strides, towards his design
Moves like a ghost. Thou sure and firm-set earth,
Hear not my steps which way they walk, for fear
Thy very stones prate of my whereabout
And take the present horror from the time,
Which now suits with it. Whiles I threat, he lives;
Words to the heat of deeds too cold breath gives.
[A bell rings.]
I go, and it is done. The bell invites me.
Hear it not, Duncan, for it is a knell
That summons thee to heaven, or to hell.

THE CONJURER'S REVENGE

Stephen Leacock

Stephen Leacock was one of the most popular humorists of the early twentieth century. This is one of his popular pieces from Literary Lapses, *published in 1910, about a stage magician who exacts his revenge on a person in the audience who keeps interrupting his show and ridiculing him. Speak the piece with the flamboyance of a magician, using the stage whisper to good effect.*

'Now, ladies and gentlemen,' said the conjurer, 'having shown you that the cloth is absolutely empty, I will proceed to take from it a bowl of goldfish. Presto!'

All around the hall people were saying, 'Oh, how wonderful! How does he do it?'

But the Quick Man on the front seat said in a big whisper to the people near him, 'He-had-it-up-his-sleeve.'

Then the people nodded brightly at the Quick Man and said, 'Oh, of course'; and everybody whispered round the hall, 'He-had-it-up-his-sleeve.'

'My next trick,' said the conjurer, 'is the famous Hindostanee rings. You will notice that the rings are apparently separate; at a blow they all join (clang, clang, clang)—Presto!'

There was a general buzz of stupefaction till the Quick Man was heard to whisper, 'He-must-have-had-another-lot-up-his-sleeve.'

Again everybody nodded and whispered, 'The-rings-were-up-his-sleeve.'

The brow of the conjurer was clouded with a gathering frown.

'I will now,' he continued, 'show you a most amusing trick by which I am enabled to take any number of eggs from a hat. Will some gentleman kindly lend me his hat? Ah, thank you—Presto!'

He extracted seventeen eggs, and for thirty-five seconds the audience began to think that he was wonderful. Then the Quick Man whispered along the front bench, 'He-has-a-hen-up-his-sleeve,' and all the people whispered it on. 'He-has-a-lot-of-hens-up-his-sleeve.'

The egg trick was ruined.

It transpired from the whispers of the Quick Man that the conjurer must have concealed up his sleeve, in addition to the rings, hens and fish, several packs of cards, a loaf of bread, a doll's cradle, a live guinea-pig, a fifty-cent piece, and a rocking-chair.

The reputation of the conjurer was rapidly sinking below zero. At the close of the evening he rallied for a final effort.

'Ladies and gentlemen,' he said, 'I will present to you, in

conclusion, the famous Japanese trick recently invented by the natives of Tipperary. Will you, sir,' he continued turning toward the Quick Man, 'will you kindly hand me your gold watch?'

It was passed to him.

'Have I your permission to put it into this mortar and pound it to pieces?' he asked savagely.

The Quick Man nodded and smiled.

The conjurer threw the watch into the mortar and grasped a sledge hammer from the table. There was a sound of violent smashing, 'He's-slipped-it-up-his-sleeve,' whispered the Quick Man.

'Now, sir,' continued the conjurer, 'will you allow me to take your handkerchief and punch holes in it? Thank you. You see, ladies and gentlemen, there is no deception; the holes are visible to the eye.'

The face of the Quick Man beamed. This time the real mystery of the thing fascinated him.

'And now, sir, will you kindly pass me your silk hat and allow me to dance on it? Thank you.'

The conjurer made a few rapid passes with his feet and exhibited the hat crushed beyond recognition.

'And will you now, sir, take off your celluloid collar and permit me to burn it in the candle? Thank you, sir. And will you allow me to smash your spectacles for you with my hammer? Thank you.'

By this time the features of the Quick Man were assuming a puzzled expression. 'This thing beats me,' he whispered, 'I don't see through it a bit.'

There was a great hush upon the audience. Then the conjurer drew himself up to his full height and, with a withering look at the Quick Man, he concluded:

'Ladies and gentlemen, you will observe that I have, with this gentleman's permission, broken his watch, burnt his collar, smashed his spectacles, and danced on his hat. If he will give me the further permission to paint green stripes on his overcoat, or to tie his suspenders in a knot, I shall be delighted to entertain you. If not, the performance is at an end.'

And amid a glorious burst of music from the orchestra the curtain fell, and the audience dispersed, convinced that there are some tricks, at any rate, that are not done up the conjurer's sleeve.

TRAIL OF THE GREEN BLAZER

R. K. Narayan

R. K. Narayan, along with Mulk Raj Anand and Raja Rao, is one of the three leading early Indian writers in English. This story is taken from Malgudi Days, *his collection of short stories set in the fictional town of Malgudi. 'Trail of the Green Blazer' is an ironic story about how Raju, a pickpocket, gets caught not when he picks pockets, but instead when he has a change of heart and tries to return the wallet to the rightful owner. I just love the way R. K. Narayan tells his stories. The bazaar comes alive with his vivid description and that is the art that you must master—to tell the story like Narayan tells it.*

The Green Blazer stood out prominently under the bright sun and blue sky. In all that jostling crowd one could not help noticing it. Villagers in shirts and turbans, townsmen in coats and caps, beggars bare-bodied, and women in multi-coloured saris were thronging the narrow passage between the stalls, and moving in great confused masses, but still the Green Blazer could not be missed. The jabber and babble of the market place was there, as people harangued, disputed prices, haggled, or greeted each other; over it all boomed the voice of a Bible-preacher and, when he paused for breath, from another corner the loudspeaker of a health van amplified on malaria and tuberculosis. Over and above it all the Green Blazer seemed to cry out an invitation. Raju could not ignore it. It was not in his nature to ignore such a persistent invitation. He kept himself half-aloof from the crowd: he could not afford to remain completely aloof nor keep himself in it too conspicuously. Wherever he might be he was harrowed by the fear of being spotted by a policeman: today he wore a loincloth and was barebodied, and had wound an enormous turban over his head, which overshadowed his face completely, and he hoped that he would be taken for a peasant from a village.

He sat on a stack of cast-off banana stalks beside a shop awning and watched the crowd. When he watched a crowd he did it with concentration. It was his professional occupation. Constitutionally he was an idler and had just the amount of energy to watch in a crowd and put his hand into another person's pocket. It was a gamble, of course. Sometimes he got nothing out of a venture, counting himself lucky if he came out with his fingers intact. Sometimes he picked up a fountain pen, and the 'receiver' behind the Municipal Office would not offer even four annas for it, and there was always the danger of being traced through it. Raju promised himself that some day he would leave fountain pens alone: he wouldn't touch one even if they were presented to him on a plate: they were too much bother—inky, leaky, and next to worthless if one could believe what the 'receiver' said about them. Watches were in the same category, too.

What Raju loved most was a nice, bulging purse. If he

saw one he picked it up with the greatest deftness. He took the cash in it, flung it far away, and went home with the satisfaction that he had done his day's job well. He splashed a little water over his face and hair and tidied himself up before walking down the street again as a normal citizen. He bought sweets, books and slates for his children, and occasionally a jacket-piece for his wife, too. He was not always easy in mind about his wife. When he went home with too much cash, he had always to take care to hide it in an envelope and shove it under a roof tile. Otherwise she asked too many questions and made herself miserable. She liked to believe that he was reformed and earned the cash he showed her as commission; she never bothered to ask what the commissions were for; a commission seemed to her something absolute.

Raju jumped down from the banana stack and followed the Green Blazer, always keeping himself three steps behind. It was a nicely calculated distance, acquired by intuition and practice. The distance must not be so much as to obscure the movement of the other's hand to and from his purse, nor so close as to become a nuisance and create suspicion. It had to be finely balanced and calculated—the same sort of calculations as carry a shikari through his tracking of game and see him safely home again. Only this hunter's task was more complicated. The hunter in the forest could count his day a success if he laid his quarry flat; but here one had to extract the heart out of the quarry without injuring it.

Raju waited patiently, pretending to be examining some rolls of rush mat, while the Green Blazer spent a considerable length of time drinking a coconut at a nearby booth. It looked as though he would not move again at all. After sucking all the water in the coconut, he seemed to wait interminably for the nut to be split and the soft white kernel scooped out with a knife. The sight of the white kernel scooped and disappearing into the other's mouth made Raju too crave for it. But he suppressed the thought: it would be inept to be spending one's time drinking and eating while one was professionally occupied; the other might slip away and be lost forever... Raju saw the other take out his black purse and start a debate with the coconut-seller over the price of coconuts. He had a thick, sawing voice which disconcerted Raju. It sounded like the growl of a tiger, but what jungle-hardened hunter ever took a step back because a tiger's growl sent his heart racing involuntarily! The way the other haggled didn't appeal to Raju either, it showed a mean and petty temperament...too much fondness for money.

Those were the narrow-minded troublemakers who made endless fuss when a purse was lost... The Green Blazer moved after all. He stopped before a stall flying coloured balloons. He bought a balloon after an endless argument with the shop man—a further demonstration of his meanness. He said: 'This is for a motherless boy. I have promised it him. If it bursts or gets lost before I go home, he will cry all night, and I wouldn't like it at all.'

Raju got his chance when the other passed through a narrow stile, where people were passing four-thick in order to see a wax model of Mahatma Gandhi reading a newspaper.

Fifteen minutes later Raju was examining the contents of the purse. He went away to a secluded spot, behind a disused well. Its crumbling parapet seemed to offer an ideal screen for his activities. The purse contained ten rupees in cash and twenty in currency notes and a few annas in nickel. Raju tucked the annas at his waist in his loincloth. 'Must give them to some beggars,' he reflected generously. There was a blind fellow yelling his life out at the entrance to the fair and nobody seemed to care. People seemed to have lost all sense of sympathy these days. The thirty rupees he bundled into a knot at the end of his turban and wrapped this again round his head. It would see him through the rest of the month. He could lead a clean life for at least a fortnight and take his wife and children to a picture.

Now the purse lay limp within the hollow of his hand. It was only left for him to fling it into the well and dust it off his hand and then he might walk among princes with equal pride at heart. He peeped into the well. It had a little shallow water at the bottom. The purse might float and a floating purse could cause the worst troubles on earth. He opened the flap of the purse in order to fill it up with pebbles before drowning it. Now, through the slit at its side, he saw a balloon folded and tucked away. 'Oh, this he bought…' He remembered the other's talk about the motherless child. 'What a fool to keep this in the purse,' Raju reflected. 'It is the carelessness of parents that makes young ones suffer,' he ruminated angrily. For a moment he paused over a picture of the growling father returning home and the motherless one waiting at the door for the promised balloon, and this growling man feeling for his purse…and, oh! it was too painful!

Raju almost sobbed at the thought of the disappointed child—the motherless boy. There was no one to comfort him. Perhaps this ruffian would beat him if he cried too long. The Green Blazer did not look like one who knew the language of children. Raju was filled with pity at the thought of the young child—perhaps of the same age as his second son. Suppose his wife were dead…(personally it might make things easier for him, he need not conceal his cash under the roof), he overcame this thought as an unworthy side-issue. If his wife should die it would make him very sad indeed and tax all his ingenuity to keep his young ones quiet... That motherless boy must have his balloon at any cost, Raju decided. But how? He peeped over the parapet across the intervening space at the crowd afar off. The balloon could not be handed back. The thing to do was to put it back into the empty purse and slip it into the other's pocket.

The Green Blazer was watching the heckling that was going on as the Bible-preacher was warming up to his subject. A semicircle was asking: 'Where is your God?' There was a hubbub. Raju sidled up to the Green Blazer. The purse with the balloon (only) tucked into it was in his palm. He'd slip it back into the other's pocket.

Raju realized his mistake in a moment. The Green Blazer caught hold of his arm and cried: 'Pickpocket!' The hecklers lost interest in the Bible and turned their attention to Raju, who tried to look appropriately outraged. He cried: 'Let me go.' The other, without giving a clue to what he proposed, shot out his arm and hit him on the cheek. It almost blinded him. For a fraction of a second Raju lost his awareness of where and even who he was. When the dark mist lifted and he was able to regain his vision, the first figure he noticed in the foreground was of the Green Blazer, looming, as it seemed, over the whole landscape. His arms were raised ready to strike again. Raju cowered at the sight. He said: 'I...I was trying to put back your purse.' The other gritted his teeth in fiendish merriment and crushed the bones of his arm. The crowd roared with laughter and badgered him. Somebody hit him again on the head.

Even before the magistrate Raju kept saying: 'I was only trying to put back the purse.' And everyone laughed. It became a stock joke in the police world. Raju's wife came to see him in jail and said, 'You have brought shame on us,' and wept.

Raju replied indignantly: 'Why? I was only trying to put it back.'

He served his term of eighteen months and came back into the world—not quite decided what he should do with himself. He told himself; 'If ever I pick up something again, I shall make sure I don't have to put it back.' For now he believed God had gifted the likes of him with only one-way deftness. Those fingers were not meant to put anything back.

Speeches

A TRYST WITH DESTINY

Jawaharlal Nehru

Jawaharlal Nehru was an exceptional speaker. This speech, made to the Indian Constituent Assembly on the eve of India's independence, close to midnight on 14 August 1947, is arguably one of the finest and most memorable speeches made in modern India.

Long years ago we made a tryst with destiny, and now the time comes when we shall redeem our pledge, not wholly or in full measure, but very substantially. At the stroke of the midnight hour, when the world sleeps, India will awake to life and freedom. A moment comes, which comes but rarely in history, when we step out from the old to the new, when an age ends, and when the soul of a nation, long suppressed, finds utterance. It is fitting that at this solemn moment, we take the pledge of dedication to the service of India and her people and to the still larger cause of humanity.

At the dawn of history, India started on her unending quest, and trackless centuries are filled with her striving and grandeur of her success and failures. Through good and ill fortune alike, she has never lost sight of that quest or forgotten the ideals which gave her strength. We end today a period of misfortunes and India discovers herself again. The achievement we celebrate today is but a step, an opening of opportunity to the greater triumphs and achievements that await us. Are we brave enough and wise enough to grasp this opportunity and accept the challenge of the future?

Freedom and power bring responsibility. The responsibility rests upon this Assembly, a sovereign body representing the sovereign people of India. Before the birth of freedom, we have endured all the pains of labour and our hearts are heavy with the memory of this sorrow. Some of those pains continue even now. Nevertheless, the past is over and it is the future that beckons us now.

That future is not one of ease or resting but of incessant striving so that we may fulfill the pledges we have so often taken and the one we shall take today. The service of India means, the service of the millions who suffer. It means the ending of poverty and ignorance and disease and inequality of opportunity. The ambition of the greatest man of our generation has been to wipe every tear from every eye. That may be beyond us, but as long as there are tears and suffering, so long our work will not be over.

And so we have to labour and to work, and to work hard, to give reality to our dreams. Those dreams are for India, but they are also for the world, for all the nations and peoples are too closely knit together today for any one of them to imagine that it can live apart. Peace is said to be indivisible, so is freedom, so is prosperity now, and also is disaster in this one world that can no longer be split into isolated fragments.

THE LIGHT HAS GONE OUT OF OUR LIVES

Jawaharlal Nehru

Perhaps one of the greatest impromptu speeches ever made, this message to the people of India on the death of Mahatma Gandhi was delivered on 30 January 1948. Spoken from the heart, it shows the poise and delivery of an expert orator. Bring out the emotion and extreme sadness of the occasion through your voice. Do not try to copy how Nehru spoke, be yourself yet speak it from the heart.

Friends and Comrades,

The light has gone out of our lives and there is darkness everywhere. I do not know what to tell you and how to say it. Our beloved leader, Bapu as we called him, the Father of the Nation, is no more. Perhaps I am wrong to say that. Nevertheless, we will never see him again as we have seen him for these many years. We will not run to him for advice and seek solace from him, and that is a terrible blow, not to me only, but to millions and millions in this country. And it is a little difficult to soften the blow by any other advice that I or anyone else can give you.

The light has gone out, I said, and yet I was wrong. For the light that shone in this country was no ordinary light. The light that has illumined this country for these many years will illumine this country for many more years, and a thousand years later, that light will be seen in this country and the world will see it and it will give solace to innumerable hearts. For that light represented something more than the immediate past, it represented the living, the eternal truths, reminding us of the right path, drawing us from error, taking this ancient country to freedom.

All this has happened when there was so much more for him to do. We could never think that he was unnecessary or that he had done his task. But now, particularly, when we are faced with so many difficulties, his not being with us is a blow most terrible to bear.

A madman has put an end to his life, for I can only call him mad who did it, and yet there has been enough of poison spread in this country during the past years and months, and this poison has had an effect on people's minds. We must face this poison, we must root out this poison, and we must face all the perils that encompass us, and face them not madly or badly, but rather in the way that our beloved teacher taught us to face them.

The first thing to remember now is that none of us dare misbehave because he is angry. We have to behave like strong and determined people, determined to face all the perils that surround us, determined to carry out the mandate that our great teacher and our great leader has given us, remembering always that if, as I believe, his spirit looks upon us and sees us, nothing would displease his soul so much as to see that we have indulged in any small behavior or any violence.

So we must not do that. But that does not mean that we should be weak, but rather that we should, in strength and in unity, face all the troubles that are in front of us. We must hold together, and all our petty troubles and difficulties and conflicts must be ended in the face of this great disaster. A great disaster is a symbol to us to remember all the big things of life and forget the small things of which we have thought too much. In his death he has reminded us of the big things of life, the living truth, and if we remember that, then it will be well with India…

It was proposed by some friends that Mahatmaji's body should be embalmed for a few days to enable millions of people to pay their last homage to him. But it was his wish, repeatedly expressed, that no such thing should happen, that this should not be done, that he was entirely opposed to any embalming of his body, and so we decided that we must follow his wishes in this matter, however much others might have wished otherwise.

And so the cremation will take place on Saturday in Delhi

city by the side of the Jamuna River. On Saturday forenoon, about 11.30 a.m., the bier will be taken out at Birla House and it will follow a prescribed road and go to the Jamuna River. The cremation will take place there at about 4 p.m. The place and the route will be announced by radio and the press.

People in Delhi who wish to pay their last homage should gather along this route. I will not advise too many of them to come to Birla House, but rather to gather on both sides of this long route from Birla House to the Jamuna River. And I trust that they will remain there in silence without any demonstrations. That is the best way and the most fitting way to pay homage to this great soul. Also, Saturday should be a day of fasting and prayer for all of us.

Those who live elsewhere, out of Delhi and in other parts of India, will no doubt take such part as they can in this last homage. For them also, let this be a day of fasting and prayer. And at the appointed time for cremation, that is 4 p.m. on Saturday afternoon, people should go to the river or to the sea and offer prayers there. And while we pray, the greatest prayer that we can offer is to take a pledge to dedicate ourselves to the truth, and to the cause for which this great countryman of ours lived and for which he has died. That is the best prayer that we can offer him and his memory. That is the best prayer we can offer to India and ourselves. Jai Hind.

SISTERS AND BROTHERS OF AMERICA

Swami Vivekananda

Swami Vivekananda was a major force in introducing Indian philosophies to the Western world. This is his famous address on the opening day of the World's Parliament of Religions in Chicago, on 11 September 1893. His opening line, 'Sisters and Brothers of America', was followed by a spontaneous applause that lasted two minutes. Say this speech from your heart and speak it with feeling; it is a winner.

Sisters and Brothers of America,

It fills my heart with joy unspeakable to rise in response to the warm and cordial welcome which you have given us. I thank you in the name of the most ancient order of monks in the world. I thank you in the name of the mother of religions, and I thank you in the name of millions and millions of Hindu people of all classes and sects.

My thanks also to some of the speakers on this platform who, referring to the delegates from the Orient, have told you that these men from far-off nations may well claim the honour of bearing to different lands the idea of toleration. I am proud to belong to a religion which has taught the world both tolerance and universal acceptance. We believe not only in universal toleration but we accept all religions as true.

I am proud to belong to a nation which has sheltered the persecuted and the refugees of all religions and all nations of the earth. I am proud to tell you that we have gathered in our bosom the purest remnant of the Israelites, who came to Southern India and took refuge with us in the very year in which their holy temple was shattered to pieces by

Roman tyranny. I am proud to belong to the religion which has sheltered and is still fostering the remnant of the grand Zoroastrian nation.

I will quote to you, brethren, a few lines from a hymn which I remember to have repeated from my earliest boyhood, and which is every day repeated by millions of human beings:

> As the different streams having their sources in different places all mingle their water in the sea, so, O Lord, the different paths which people take through different tendencies, various though they appear, crooked or straight, all lead to Thee.

The present convention, which is one of the most august assemblies ever held, is in itself a vindication, a declaration to the world of the wonderful doctrine preached in the Gita:

> Whosoever comes to Me, through whatsoever form, I reach them; all are struggling through paths which in the end lead to Me.

Sectarianism, bigotry, and its horrible descendant, fanaticism, have long possessed this beautiful earth. They have filled the earth with violence, drenched it often and often with human blood, destroyed civilization and sent whole nations to despair. Had it not been for these horrible demons, human society would be far more advanced than it is now. But their time is come; and I fervently hope that the bell that tolled this morning in honour of this convention may be the death-knell of all fanaticism, of all persecutions with the sword or with the pen, and of all uncharitable feelings between persons wending their way to the same goal.

QUIT INDIA
Mahatma Gandhi

Mahatma Gandhi made a number of memorable speeches. This speech was made at Gowalia Tank Maidan in Bombay, on 8 August 1942. This masterful speech, calling for determined but passive resistance, motivated a large number of Indians to join the Quit India movement. Speak with the conviction of one determined to succeed and who believes in every word he says.

Before you discuss the resolution, let me place before you one or two things, I want you to understand two things very clearly and to consider them from the same point of view from which I am placing them before you. I ask you to consider it from my point of view, because if you approve of it, you will be enjoined to carry out all I say. It will be a great responsibility. There are people who ask me whether I am the same man that I was in 1920, or whether there has been any change in me. You are right in asking that question.

Let me, however, hasten to assure that I am the same Gandhi as I was in 1920. I have not changed in any fundamental respect. I attach the same importance to non-violence that I did then. If at all, my emphasis on it has grown stronger. There is no real contradiction between the present resolution and my previous writings and utterances.

Occasions like the present do not occur in everybody's and but rarely in anybody's life. I want you to know and feel that there is nothing but purest Ahimsa in all that I am saying and doing today. The draft resolution of the Working Committee is based on Ahimsa, the contemplated struggle similarly has its roots in Ahimsa. If, therefore, there is any among you who has lost faith in Ahimsa or is wearied of it, let him not vote for this resolution.

Let me explain my position clearly. God has vouchsafed to me a priceless gift in the weapon of Ahimsa. I and my Ahimsa are on our trail today. If in the present crisis, when the earth is being scorched by the flames of Himsa and crying for deliverance, I failed to make use of the God given talent, God will not forgive me and I shall be judged un-wrongly of the great gift. I must act now. I may not hesitate and merely look on, when Russia and China are threatened.

Ours is not a drive for power, but purely a non-violent fight for India's independence. In a violent struggle, a successful general has been often known to effect a military coup and to set up a dictatorship. But under the Congress scheme of things, essentially non-violent as it is, there can be no room for dictatorship. A non-violent soldier of freedom will covet nothing for himself; he fights only for the freedom of his country. The Congress is unconcerned as to who will rule, when freedom is attained. The power, when it comes, will belong to the people of India, and it will be for them to decide to whom it placed in the entrusted. May be that the reins will be placed in the hands of the Parsis, for instance—as I would love to see happen—or they may be handed to some others whose names are not heard in the Congress today. It will not be for you then to object saying, 'This community is microscopic. That party did not play its due part in the freedom's struggle; why should it have all the power?' Ever since its inception the Congress has kept itself meticulously free of the communal taint. It has thought always in terms of the whole nation and has acted accordingly...

I know how imperfect our Ahimsa is and how far away we are still from the ideal, but in Ahimsa there is no final failure or defeat. I have faith, therefore, that if, in spite of our shortcomings, the big thing does happen, it will be because God wanted to help us by crowning with success our silent, unremitting Sadhana for the last twenty-two years.

I believe that in the history of the world, there has not been a more genuinely democratic struggle for freedom than ours. I read Carlyle's *French Revolution* while I was in prison, and Pandit Jawaharlal has told me something about the Russian revolution. But it is my conviction that inasmuch as these struggles were fought with the weapon of violence they failed to realize the democratic ideal. In the democracy which I have envisaged, a democracy established by non-violence, there will be equal freedom for all. Everybody will be his own master. It is to join a struggle for such democracy that I invite you today. Once you realize this you will forget the differences between the Hindus and Muslims, and think of yourselves as Indians only, engaged in the common struggle for independence.

Then, there is the question of your attitude towards the British. I have noticed that there is hatred towards the British among the people. The people say they are disgusted with their behaviour. The people make no distinction between British imperialism and the British people. To them, the two are one. This hatred would even make them welcome the Japanese. It is most dangerous. It means that they will exchange one slavery for another. We must get rid of this feeling. Our quarrel is not with the British people, we fight their imperialism. The proposal for the withdrawal of British power did not come out of anger. It came to enable India to play its due part at the present critical juncture It is not a happy position for a big country like India to be merely helping with money and material obtained willy-nilly from her while the United

Nations are conducting the war. We cannot evoke the true spirit of sacrifice and valour, so long as we are not free. I know the British Government will not be able to withhold freedom from us, when we have made enough self-sacrifice. We must, therefore, purge ourselves of hatred. Speaking for myself, I can say that I have never felt any hatred. As a matter of fact, I feel myself to be a greater friend of the British now than ever before. One reason is that they are today in distress. My very friendship, therefore, demands that I should try to save them from their mistakes. As I view the situation, they are on the brink of an abyss. It, therefore, becomes my duty to warn them of their danger even though it may, for the time being, anger them to the point of cutting off the friendly hand that is stretched out to help them. People may laugh, nevertheless that is my claim. At a time when I may have to launch the biggest struggle of my life, I may not harbour hatred against anybody.

YES WE CAN CHANGE

Barack Obama

This is Barack Obama's victory speech after he won the Democratic presidential primary in South Carolina on 26 January 2008. 'Yes we can' went on to become a popular slogan of his presidential campaign, which as we all know he went on to win convincingly. A winning piece if you can deliver it well...yes you can!

Over two weeks ago, we saw the people of Iowa proclaim that our time for change has come. But there were those who doubted this country's desire for something new, who said Iowa was a fluke, not to be repeated again.

Well, tonight, the cynics who believed that what began in the snows of Iowa was just an illusion were told a different story by the good people of South Carolina.

After four great contests, in every corner of this country, we have the most votes, the most delegates, and the most diverse coalition of Americans that we've seen in a long, long time. You can see it in the faces here tonight. There are young and old, rich and poor. There are black and white, Latino and Asian and Native American. And we've got young people all across this country who have never had a reason to participate until now.

And in nine days, in nine short days, nearly half the nation will have the chance to join us in saying that we are tired of business as usual in Washington. We are hungry for change and we are ready to believe again.

But if there's anything, though, that we have been reminded of since Iowa, it's that the kind of change we seek will not come easy, partly because we have fine candidates in this, fierce competitors who are worthy of our respect and our admiration. And as contentious as this campaign may get, we have to remember that this is a contest for the Democratic nomination. And that all of us share an abiding desire to end the disastrous policies of the current administration.

But there are real differences between the candidates. We are looking for more than just a change of party in the White House. We're looking to fundamentally change the status quo in Washington.

It's a status quo that extends beyond any particular party and right now that status quo is fighting back with everything it's got, with the same old tactics that divide and distract us from solving the problems people face, whether those problems are health care that folks can't afford or a mortgage they cannot pay.

So this will not be easy. Make no mistake about what we're up against. We're up against the belief that it's all right for lobbyists to dominate our government, that they are just part of the system in Washington. But we know that the undue influence of lobbyists is part of the problem and this election is our chance to say that we are not going to let them stand in our way anymore.

We're up against the conventional thinking that says your ability to lead as president comes from longevity in Washington or proximity to the White House. But we know that real leadership is about candour and judgement and the ability to rally Americans from all walks of life around a common purpose, a higher purpose.

We're up against decades of bitter partisanship that cause politicians to demonize their opponents instead of coming together to make college affordable or energy cleaner. It's the kind of partisanship where you're not even allowed to say that a Republican had an idea, even if it's one you never agreed with. That's the kind of politics that is bad for our party, it is bad for our country, and this is our chance to end it once and for all.

We're up against the idea that it's acceptable to say anything and do anything to win an election. But we know that this is exactly what's wrong with our politics. This is why people don't believe what their leaders say anymore. This is why they tune out. And this election is our chance to give the American people a reason to believe again.

But let me say this, South Carolina. What we've seen in these last weeks is that we're also up against forces that are not the fault of any one campaign, but feed the habits that prevent us from being who we want to be as a nation.

It's the politics that uses religion as a wedge and patriotism as a bludgeon, a politics that tells us that we have to think, act and even vote within the confines of the categories that supposedly define us, the assumption that young people are apathetic, the assumption that Republicans won't cross over, the assumption that the wealthy care nothing for the poor and that the poor don't vote, the assumption that African Americans can't support the white candidate, whites can't support the African American candidate, blacks and Latinos cannot come together.

We are here tonight to say that that is not the America we believe in. I did not travel around this state over the last year and see a white South Carolina or a black South Carolina. I saw South Carolina. I saw crumbling schools that are stealing the future of black children and white children alike. I saw shuttered mills and homes for sale that once belonged to Americans from all walks of life and men and women of every colour and creed who serve together and fight together and bleed together under the same proud flag.

I saw what America is and I believe in what this country can be. That is the country I see. That is the country you see. But now it is up to us to help the entire nation embrace this vision.

Because in the end, we're not just against the ingrained and destructive habits of Washington, we're also struggling with our own doubts, our own fears, our own cynicism.

The change we seek has always required great struggle and great sacrifice. And so this is a battle in our own hearts and minds about what kind of country we want and how hard we're willing to work for it.

So let me remind you tonight that change will not be easy. Change will take time. There will be setbacks and false starts and sometimes we'll make mistakes.

But as hard as it may seem, we cannot lose hope, because there are people all across this great nation who are counting on us, who can't afford another four years without health care, that can't afford another four years without good schools, that can't afford another four years without decent wages because our leaders couldn't come together and get it done.

Theirs are the stories and voices we carry on from South Carolina. The mother who can't get Medicaid to cover all the needs of her sick child. She needs us to pass a health care plan that cuts costs and makes health care available and affordable for every single American. That's what she's looking for.

The teacher who works another shift at Dunkin Donuts after school just to make ends meet, she needs us to reform our education system so that she gets better pay and more support and her students get the resources that they need to achieve their dreams.

The Maytag worker who's now competing with his own teenager for a $7-an-hour job at the local Wal-Mart, because the factory he gave his life to shut its doors, he needs us to stop giving tax breaks to companies that ship our jobs overseas and start putting them in the pockets of working Americans who deserve it and put them in the pockets of struggling homeowners who are having a tough time and looking after seniors who should retire with dignity and respect.

The woman who told me that she hasn't been able to breathe since the day her nephew left for Iraq or the soldier who doesn't know his child because he's on his third or fourth or even fifth tour of duty, they need us to come together and put an end to a war that should have never been authorized and should have never been waged.

So understand this, South Carolina. The choice in this election is not between regions or religions or genders. It's not about rich versus poor, young versus old. And it is not about black versus white. This election is about the past versus the future.

It's about whether we settle for the same divisions and distractions and drama that passes for politics today or whether we reach for a politics of common sense and innovation, a politics of shared sacrifice and shared prosperity.

There are those who will continue to tell us that we can't do this, that we can't have what we're looking for, that we can't have what we want, that we're peddling false hopes. But here is what I know. I know that when people say we can't overcome all the big money and influence in Washington, I think of that elderly woman who sent me a contribution the other day, an envelope that had a money order for $3.01, along with a verse of scripture tucked inside the envelope. So don't tell us change isn't possible. That woman knows change is possible.

When I hear the cynical talk that blacks and whites and Latinos can't join together and work together, I'm reminded of the Latino brothers and sisters I organized with and stood with and fought with side by side for jobs and justice on the streets of Chicago. So don't tell us change can't happen.

When I hear that we'll never overcome the racial divide in our politics, I think about that Republican woman who used to work for Strom Thurmond, who is now devoted to educating inner city children and who went out into the streets of South Carolina and knocked on doors for this campaign.

Don't tell me we can't change. Yes, we can.

Yes, we can change. Yes, we can heal this nation. Yes, we can seize our future.

And as we leave this great state with a new wind at our backs and we take this journey across this great country, a country we love, with the message we carry from the plains of Iowa to the hills of New Hampshire, from the Nevada desert to the South Carolina coast, the same message we had when we were up and when we were down, that out of many, we are one; that while we breathe, we will hope.

And where we are met with cynicism and doubt and fear and those who tell us that we can't, we will respond with that timeless creed that sums up the spirit of the American people in three simple words: Yes We Can.

GIVE ME LIBERTY OR GIVE ME DEATH!

Patrick Henry

Patrick Henry was a founding father of the United States of America. He was a lawyer, politician and skilled orator. This is an extract from a speech made on 23 March 1775 in which he was convincing the Virginia House of Burgesses to pass a resolution to send the Virginia troops to the Revolutionary War. Among the delegates to the convention were two future US presidents, Thomas Jefferson and George Washington.

I have but one lamp by which my feet are guided, and that is the lamp of experience. I know of no way of judging of the future but by the past. And judging by the past, I wish to know what there has been in the conduct of the British ministry for the last ten years to justify those hopes with which gentlemen have been pleased to solace themselves and the House. Is it that insidious smile with which our petition has been lately received? Trust it not, sir; it will prove a snare to your feet. Suffer not yourselves to be betrayed with a kiss. Ask yourselves how this gracious reception of our petition comports with those warlike preparations which cover our waters and darken our land. Are fleets and armies necessary to a work of love and reconciliation? Have we shown ourselves so unwilling to be reconciled that force must be called in to win back our love? Let us not deceive ourselves, sir. These are the implements of war and subjugation; the last arguments to which kings resort. I ask gentlemen, sir, what means this martial array, if its purpose be not to force us to submission? Can gentlemen assign any other possible motive for it? Has Great Britain any enemy, in this quarter of the world, to call for all this accumulation of navies and armies? No, sir, she has none. They are meant for us: they can be meant for no other. They are sent over to bind and rivet upon us those chains which the British ministry has been so long forging. And what have we to oppose to them? Shall we try argument? Sir, we have been trying that for the last ten years. Have we anything new to offer upon the subject? Nothing. We have held the subject up in every light of which it is capable; but it has been all in vain. Shall we resort to entreaty and humble supplication? What terms shall we find which have not been already exhausted? Let us not, I beseech you, sir, deceive ourselves. Sir, we have done everything that could be done to avert the storm which is now coming on. We have petitioned; we have remonstrated; we have supplicated; we have prostrated ourselves before the throne, and have implored its interposition to arrest the tyrannical hands of the ministry and Parliament. Our petitions have been slighted; our remonstrances have produced additional violence and insult; our supplications have been disregarded; and we have been spurned, with contempt, from the foot of the throne! In vain, after these things, may we indulge the fond hope of peace and reconciliation. There is no longer any room for hope. If we wish to be free—if we mean to preserve inviolate those inestimable privileges for which we have been so long contending—if we mean not basely to abandon the noble struggle in which we have been so long engaged, and which we have pledged ourselves never to abandon until the glorious object of our contest shall be obtained—we must fight! I repeat it, sir, we must fight! An appeal to arms and to the God of hosts is all that is left us!

They tell us sir, that we are weak; unable to cope with so formidable an adversary. But when shall we be stronger? Will it be the next week, or the next year? Will it be when we are totally disarmed, and when a British guard shall be stationed in every house? Shall we gather strength by irresolution and inaction? Shall we acquire the means of effectual resistance by lying supinely on our backs and hugging the delusive phantom of hope, until our enemies shall have bound us hand and foot? Sir, we are not weak if we make a proper use of those means which the God of nature hath placed in our power. The millions of people, armed in the holy cause of liberty, and in such a country as that which we possess, are invincible by any force which our enemy can send against us. Besides, sir, we shall not fight our battles alone. There is a just God who presides over the destinies of nations, and who will raise up friends to fight our battles for us. The battle, sir, is not to the strong alone; it is to the vigilant, the active, the brave. Besides, sir, we have no election. If we were base enough to desire it, it is now too late to retire from the contest. There is no retreat but in submission and slavery! Our chains are forged! Their clanking may be heard on the plains of Boston! The war is inevitable—and let it come! I repeat it, sir, let it come.

It is in vain, sir, to extenuate the matter. Gentlemen may cry, Peace, Peace—but there is no peace. The war is actually begun! The next gale that sweeps from the north will bring to our ears the clash of resounding arms! Our brethren are already in the field! Why stand we here idle? What is it that gentlemen wish? What would they have? Is life so dear, or peace so sweet, as to be purchased at the price of chains and slavery? Forbid it, Almighty God! I know not what course others may take; but as for me, give me liberty or give me death!

THEIR FINEST HOUR

Winston Churchill

Winston Churchill is considered to be one of the greatest wartime leaders. He is also remembered for his quick wit and superb oratory. This speech is one of his most stirring ones. It was delivered in the House of Commons on 18 June 1940, where he talks about how, in the Second World War, Britain has been left standing alone against Hitler's relentless march across Europe. This is a powerful and hard-hitting speech. Punctuate your delivery with a couple of 'clenched-fist punches' to drive home the important points.

I spoke the other day of the colossal military disaster which occurred when the French High Command failed to withdraw the northern armies from Belgium at the moment when they knew that the French front was decisively broken at Sedan and on the Meuse. This delay entailed the loss of fifteen or sixteen French divisions and threw out of action for the critical period the whole of the British Expeditionary Force. Our Army and 120,000 French troops were indeed rescued by the British Navy from Dunkirk but only with the loss of their cannon, vehicles and modern equipment. This loss inevitably took some weeks to repair, and in the first two of those weeks the battle in France has been lost.

Now I put all this aside. I put it on the shelf, from which the historians, when they have time, will select their documents to tell their stories. We have to think of the future and not of the past. This also applies in a small way to our own affairs at home.

Of this I am quite sure, that if we open a quarrel between the past and the present, we shall find that we have lost the future. Therefore, I cannot accept the drawing of any distinctions between members of the present government. It was formed at a moment of crisis in order to unite all the parties and all sections of opinion. Its members are going to stand together, and, subject to the authority of the House of Commons, we are going to govern the country and fight the war.

The disastrous military events which have happened during the past fortnight have not come to me with any sense of surprise. Indeed, I indicated a fortnight ago as clearly as I could to the House that the worst possibilities were open; and I made it perfectly clear then that whatever happened in France would make no difference to the resolve of Britain and the British Empire to fight on, if necessary for years, if necessary alone.

During the last few days we have successfully brought off the great majority of the troops we had on the line of communication in France; and seven-eighths of the troops we have sent to France since the beginning of the war.

We have, therefore, in this island today a very large and powerful military force. This force comprises all our best-trained and our finest troops, including scores of thousands of those who have already measured their quality against the Germans and found themselves at no disadvantage.

Lest the account which I have given of these large forces should raise the question: why did they not take part in the great battle in France? I must make it clear that, apart from the divisions training and organizing at home, only twelve divisions were equipped to fight upon a scale which justified their being sent abroad. And this was fully up to the number which the French had been led to expect would be available in France at the ninth month of the war.

Here is where we come to the Navy—and after all, we have a Navy. Some people seem to forget that we have a Navy. We must remind them. For the last thirty years I have been concerned in discussions about the possibilities of overseas invasion, and I took the responsibility on behalf of the Admiralty, at the beginning of the last war, of allowing all regular troops to be sent out of the country. We are also told that the Italian Navy is to come out and gain sea superiority in these waters. If they seriously intend it, I shall only say that we shall be delighted to offer Signor Mussolini a free and safeguarded passage through the Strait of Gibraltar in order that he may play the part to which he aspires.

Therefore, it seems to me that as far as seaborne invasion on a great scale is concerned, we are far more capable of meeting it today than we were at many periods in the last war and during the early months of this war, before our other troops were trained.

Some people will ask why, then, was it that the British Navy was not able to prevent the movement of a large army from Germany into Norway across the Skagerrak? But the conditions in the Channel and in the North Sea are in no way like those which prevail in the Skagerrak. In the Skagerrak, because of the distance, we could give no air support to our surface ships, and consequently, lying as we did close to the enemy's main air power, we were compelled to use only our submarines. Our submarines took a heavy toll but could not, by themselves, prevent the invasion of Norway. In the Channel and in the North Sea, on the other hand, our superior naval surface forces, aided by our submarines, will operate with close and effective air assistance.

This brings me, naturally, to the great question of invasion from the air, and of the impending struggle between the British and German Air Forces. The great question is: can we break Hitler's air weapon? Now, of course, it is a very great pity that we have not got an Air Force at least equal to that of the most powerful enemy within striking distance of these shores. But we have a very powerful Air Force which has proved itself far superior in quality, both in men and in many types of machine.

There remains, of course, the danger of bombing attacks, which will certainly be made very soon upon us by the bomber forces of the enemy. It is true that the German bomber force is superior in numbers to ours; but we have a very large bomber force also, which we shall use to strike at military targets in Germany without intermission. For all of us, at this time, whatever our sphere, our station, our occupation or our duties, it will be a help to remember the famous lines: he nothing common did or mean, upon that memorable scene.

I have thought it right upon this occasion to give the House and the country some indication of the solid, practical grounds upon which we base our inflexible resolve to continue the war. There are a good many people who say, 'Never mind. Win or lose, sink or swim, better die than submit to tyranny—and such a tyranny.' And I do not dissociate myself from them. But I can assure them that our professional advisers of the three Services unitedly advise that we should carry on the war, and that there are good and reasonable hopes of final victory.

We may now ask ourselves: In what way has our position worsened since the beginning of the war? It has worsened by the fact that the Germans have conquered a large part of the coast line of Western Europe.

If Hitler can bring under his despotic control the industries of the countries he has conquered, this will add greatly to his already vast armament output. On the other hand, this will not happen immediately, and we are now assured of immense, continuous and increasing support in supplies and munitions of all kinds from the United States.

Therefore, in casting up this dread balance sheet and contemplating our dangers with a disillusioned eye, I see great reason for intense vigilance and exertion, but none whatever for panic or despair.

During the first four years of the last war the Allies experienced nothing but disaster and disappointment. That was our constant fear: one blow after another, terrible losses, frightful dangers. During that war we repeatedly asked ourselves the question: 'How are we going to win?' And no one was able ever to answer it with much precision, until at the end, quite suddenly, quite unexpectedly, our terrible foe collapsed before us, and we were so glutted with victory that in our folly we threw it away.

The French government will be throwing away great opportunities and casting adrift their future if they do not continue the war in accordance with their treaty obligations, from which we have not felt able to release them. The House will have read the historic declaration in which, at the desire of many Frenchmen—and of our own hearts—we have proclaimed our willingness at the darkest hour in French history to conclude a union of common citizenship in this struggle. However matters may go in France, we will never lose our sense of comradeship with the French people. If we are now called upon to endure what they have been suffering, we shall emulate their courage, and if final victory rewards our toils they shall share the gains, aye, and freedom shall be restored to all.

What General Weygand called the Battle of France is over. I expect that the Battle of Britain is about to begin. Upon this battle depends the survival of Christian civilization. Upon it depends our own British life, and the long continuity of our institutions and our empire. The whole fury and might of the enemy must very soon be turned on us.

Hitler knows that he will have to break us in this island or lose the war. If we can stand up to him, all Europe may be free and the life of the world may move forward into broad, sunlit uplands. But if we fail, then the whole world, including the United States, including all that we have known and cared for, will sink into the abyss of a new Dark Age made more sinister, and perhaps more protracted, by the lights of perverted science.

Let us therefore brace ourselves to our duties, and so bear ourselves that if the British Empire and its Commonwealth last for a thousand years, men will still say, 'This was their finest hour.'

ASK NOT WHAT YOUR COUNTRY CAN DO FOR YOU
John F. Kennedy

John F. Kennedy was one of the youngest presidents of the United States. He made a number of moving and appealing speeches. This, one of the most famous, was his inaugural address, delivered on 20 January 1961. A good piece for senior school, but you might not score very highly in the 'choice of piece' parameter as it is very popular.

Vice President Johnson, Mr Speaker, Mr Chief Justice, President Eisenhower, Vice President Nixon, President Truman, reverend clergy, fellow citizens, we observe today not a victory of party, but a celebration of freedom—symbolizing an end, as well as a beginning—signifying renewal, as well as change. For I have sworn before you and Almighty God the same solemn oath our forebears prescribed nearly a century and three quarters ago.

The world is very different now. For man holds in his mortal hands the power to abolish all forms of human poverty and all forms of human life. And yet the same revolutionary beliefs for which our forebears fought are still at issue around the globe—the belief that the rights of man come not from the generosity of the state, but from the hand of God.

We dare not forget today that we are the heirs of that first revolution. Let the word go forth from this time and place, to friend and foe alike, that the torch has been passed to a new generation of Americans—born in this century, tempered by war, disciplined by a hard and bitter peace, proud of our ancient heritage—and unwilling to witness or permit the slow undoing of those human rights to which this nation has always been committed, and to which we are committed today at home and around the world.

Let every nation know, whether it wishes us well or ill, that we shall pay any price, bear any burden, meet any hardship, support any friend, oppose any foe, in order to assure the survival and the success of liberty.

This much we pledge—and more.

To those old allies whose cultural and spiritual origins we share, we pledge the loyalty of faithful friends. United, there is little we cannot do in a host of cooperative ventures. Divided, there is little we can do—for we dare not meet a powerful challenge at odds and split asunder.

To those new states whom we welcome to the ranks of

the free, we pledge our word that one form of colonial control shall not have passed away merely to be replaced by a far more iron tyranny. We shall not always expect to find them supporting our view. But we shall always hope to find them strongly supporting their own freedom—and to remember that, in the past, those who foolishly sought power by riding the back of the tiger ended up inside.

To those peoples in the huts and villages across the globe struggling to break the bonds of mass misery, we pledge our best efforts to help them help themselves, for whatever period is required—not because the communists may be doing it, not because we seek their votes, but because it is right. If a free society cannot help the many who are poor, it cannot save the few who are rich.

To our sister republics south of our border, we offer a special pledge—to convert our good words into good deeds—in a new alliance for progress—to assist free men and free governments in casting off the chains of poverty. But this peaceful revolution of hope cannot become the prey of hostile powers. Let all our neighbours know that we shall join with them to oppose aggression or subversion anywhere in the Americas. And let every other power know that this hemisphere intends to remain the master of its own house.

To that world assembly of sovereign states, the United Nations, our last best hope in an age where the instruments of war have far outpaced the instruments of peace, we renew our pledge of support—to prevent it from becoming merely a forum for invective—to strengthen its shield of the new and the weak—and to enlarge the area in which its writ may run.

Finally, to those nations who would make themselves our adversary, we offer not a pledge but a request: that both sides begin anew the quest for peace, before the dark powers of destruction unleashed by science engulf all humanity in planned or accidental self-destruction.

We dare not tempt them with weakness. For only when our arms are sufficient beyond doubt can we be certain beyond doubt that they will never be employed.

But neither can two great and powerful groups of nations take comfort from our present course—both sides overburdened by the cost of modern weapons, both rightly alarmed by the steady spread of the deadly atom, yet both racing to alter that uncertain balance of terror that stays the hand of mankind's final war.

So let us begin anew—remembering on both sides that civility is not a sign of weakness, and sincerity is always subject to proof. Let us never negotiate out of fear. But let us never fear to negotiate.

Let both sides explore what problems unite us instead of belabouring those problems which divide us.

Let both sides, for the first time, formulate serious and precise proposals for the inspection and control of arms—and bring the absolute power to destroy other nations under the absolute control of all nations.

Let both sides seek to invoke the wonders of science instead of its terrors. Together let us explore the stars, conquer the deserts, eradicate disease, tap the ocean depths, and encourage the arts and commerce.

Let both sides unite to heed in all corners of the earth the command of Isaiah—to 'undo the heavy burdens...and to let the oppressed go free.'

And if a beachhead of cooperation may push back the jungle of suspicion, let both sides join in creating a new endeavour, not a new balance of power, but a new world of law, where the strong are just and the weak secure and the peace preserved.

All this will not be finished in the first hundred days. Nor will it be finished in the first thousand days, nor in the life of this administration, nor even perhaps in our lifetime on this planet. But let us begin.

In your hands, my fellow citizens, more than in mine, will rest the final success or failure of our course. Since this country was founded, each generation of Americans has been summoned to give testimony to its national loyalty. The graves of young Americans who answered the call to service surround the globe.

Now the trumpet summons us again—not as a call to bear arms, though arms we need; not as a call to battle, though embattled we are—but a call to bear the burden of a long twilight struggle, year in and year out, 'rejoicing in hope, patient in tribulation'—a struggle against the common enemies of man: tyranny, poverty, disease, and war itself.

Can we forge against these enemies a grand and global alliance, North and South, East and West, that can assure a more fruitful life for all mankind? Will you join in that historic effort?

In the long history of the world, only a few generations have been granted the role of defending freedom in its hour of maximum danger. I do not shrink from this responsibility—I welcome it. I do not believe that any of us would exchange places with any other people or any other generation. The energy, the faith, the devotion which we bring to this endeavour will light our country and all who serve it—and the glow from that fire can truly light the world.

And so, my fellow Americans: ask not what your country

can do for you—ask what you can do for your country.

My fellow citizens of the world: ask not what America will do for you, but what together we can do for the freedom of man.

Finally, whether you are citizens of America or citizens of the world, ask of us the same high standards of strength and sacrifice which we ask of you. With a good conscience our only sure reward, with history the final judge of our deeds, let us go forth to lead the land we love, asking His blessing and His help, but knowing that here on earth God's work must truly be our own.

From NOBEL PRIZE LECTURE
Mother Teresa

Mother Teresa was once asked, 'What can we do to promote world peace?' She answered, 'Go home and love your family.' Here are excerpts from Mother Teresa's Nobel Peace Prize lecture delivered on 11 December 1979 in Oslo. Before you say this speech, make sure you have read about Mother Teresa and know and understand the great work she did. If you can get yourself to think the way she did, you will be able to bring the conviction into your tone.

Let us thank God for the opportunity that we all have together today, for this gift of peace that reminds us that we have been created to live that peace.

It is not enough for us to say: I love God, but I do not love my neighbour. How can you love God whom you do not see, if you do not love your neighbour whom you see, whom you touch, with whom you live. And so this is very important for us to realize that love, to be true, has to hurt.

I never forget an opportunity I had in visiting a home where they had all these old parents of sons and daughters who had just put them in an institution and forgotten maybe. And I went there, and I saw in that home they had everything, beautiful things, but everybody was looking towards the door. And I did not see a single one with their smile on their face. And I turned to the Sister and I asked: How is it that the people they have everything here, why are they all looking towards the door, why are they not smiling? I am so used to see the smile on our people, even the dying one smile, and she said: This is nearly every day, they are expecting, they are hoping that a son or daughter will come to visit them. They are hurt because they are forgotten, and see—this is where love comes.

I was surprised in the West to see so many young boys and girls given into drugs, and I tried to find out why—why is it like that, and the answer was: because there is no one in the family to receive them. Father and mother are so busy they have no time. We are talking of peace. These are things that break peace. Many people are very, very concerned with the children in India, with the children in Africa where quite a number die, maybe of malnutrition, of hunger and so on, but millions are dying deliberately by the will of the mother. And this is what is the greatest destroyer of peace today. And this I appeal in India, I appeal everywhere: let us bring the child back, and this year being the child's year: what have we done for the child.

The poor people are very great people. They can teach us so many beautiful things. The other day one of them came to thank and said: You people who have vowed chastity you are the best people to teach us family planning. Because it is nothing more than self-control out of love for each other. And

I think they said a beautiful sentence. And these are people who maybe have nothing to eat, maybe they have not a home where to live, but they are great people. The poor are very wonderful people. One evening we went out and we picked up four people from the street. And one of them was in a most terrible condition—and I told the Sisters: You take care of the other three, I take of this one that looked worse. So I did for her all that my love can do. I put her in bed, and there was such a beautiful smile on her face. She took hold of my hand, as she said one word only: Thank you—and she died.

I could not help but examine my conscience before her, and I asked what would I say if I was in her place. And my answer was very simple. I would have tried to draw a little attention to myself, I would have said I am hungry, that I am dying, I am cold, I am in pain, or something, but she gave me much more—she gave me her grateful love. And she died with a smile on her face. As that man whom we picked up from the drain, half eaten with worms, and we brought him to the home. I have lived like an animal in the street, but I am going to die like an angel, loved and cared for. And it was so wonderful to see the greatness of that man who could speak like that, who could die like that without blaming anybody, without cursing anybody, without comparing anything.

I believe that we are not real social workers. We may be doing social work in the eyes of the people, but we are really contemplatives in the heart of the world. And I think that we in our family don't need bombs and guns, to destroy to bring peace—just get together, love one another, bring that peace, that joy, that strength of presence of each other in the home. And we will be able to overcome all the evil that is in the world.

There is so much suffering, so much hatred, so much misery, and we with our prayer, with our sacrifice are beginning at home. Love begins at home, and it is not how much we do, but how much love we put in the action that we do.

Some time ago in Calcutta we had great difficulty in getting sugar, and I don't know how the word got around to the children, and a little boy of four years old, Hindu boy, went home and told his parents: I will not eat sugar for three days, I will give my sugar to Mother Teresa for her children. After three days his father and mother brought him to our home. I had never met them before, and this little one could scarcely pronounce my name, but he knew exactly what he had come to do. He knew that he wanted to share his love.

And that is why I have received such a lot of love from you all. From the time that I have come here I have simply been surrounded with love.

And so here I am talking with you—I want you to find the poor here, right in your own home first. And begin love there. Be that good news to your own people. And find out about your next-door neighbour—do you know who they are? I had the most extraordinary experience with a Hindu family who had eight children. A gentleman came to our house and said: Mother Teresa, there is a family with eight children, they had not eaten for so long—do something. So I took some rice and I went there immediately. And I saw the children—their eyes shining with hunger. I don't know if you have ever seen hunger, but I have seen it very often. And she took the rice, she divided the rice, and she went out. When she came back I asked her—where did you go, what did you do? And she gave me a very simple answer: They (her neighbours) are hungry also. What struck me most was that she knew—and who are they, a Muslim family—and she knew. I didn't bring more rice that evening because I wanted them to enjoy the joy of sharing. But there were those children, radiating joy, sharing the joy with their mother because she had the love to give. And you see this is where love begins—at home.

And I know well that you have not given from your abundance, but you have given until it has hurt you. And with this prize that I have received as a prize of peace, I am going to try to make the home for many people that have no home. Because I believe that love begins at home, and if we can create a home for the poor—I think that more and more love will spread. And we will be able through this understanding love to bring peace, be the good news to the poor.

To be able to do this, our Sisters, our lives have to be woven with prayer. They have to be woven with Christ to be able to understand, to be able to share. Because today there is so much suffering. Are we there to share that passion, to share that suffering of people? Around the world, not only in the poor countries, but I found the poverty of the West so much more difficult to remove. When I pick up a person from the street, hungry, I give him a plate of rice, a piece of bread, I have satisfied. I have removed that hunger. But a person that is shut out, that feels unwanted, unloved, terrified, the person that has been thrown out from society—that poverty is so hurtable and so much, and I find that very difficult. Our Sisters are working amongst that kind of people in the West. So you must pray for us that we may be able to be that good news, but we cannot do that without you, you have to do that here in your country.

How difficult we find it sometimes to smile at each other, and that the smile is the beginning of love. And so let us always meet each other with a smile, for the smile is the beginning of love, and once we begin to love each other naturally we want to do something.

The other day I received fifteen dollars from a man who has been on his back for twenty years, and the only part that he can move is his right hand. And the only companion that he enjoys is smoking. And he said to me: I do not smoke for one week, and I send you this money. It must have been a terrible sacrifice for him, but see how beautiful, how he shared, and with that money I bought bread and I gave to those who are hungry with a joy on both sides, he was giving and the poor were receiving. This is something that you and I—it is a gift of God to us to be able to share our love with others. And let it be as it was for Jesus. Let us love one another as He loved us. Let us love Him with undivided love. And the joy of loving Him and each other—let us give now—that Christmas is coming so close. Let us keep that joy of loving Jesus in our hearts. And share that joy with all that we come in touch with. And that radiating joy is real, for we have no reason not to be happy because we have no Christ with us. Christ in our hearts, Christ in the poor that we meet, Christ in the smile that we give and the smile that we receive. Let us make that one point: that no child will be unwanted, and also that we meet each other always with a smile, especially when it is difficult to smile.

I never forget some time ago about fourteen professors came from the United States from different universities. And they came to Calcutta to our house. Then we were talking about that they had been to the home for the dying. We have a home for the dying in Calcutta, where we have picked up more than 36,000 people only from the streets of Calcutta, and out of that big number more than 18,000 have died a beautiful death. They have just gone home to God; and they came to our house and we talked of love, of compassion, and then one of them asked me: Say, Mother, please tell us something that we will remember, and I said to them: Smile at each other, make time for each other in your family. Smile at each other. And then another one asked me: Are you married, and I said: Yes, and I find it sometimes very difficult to smile at Jesus because he can be very demanding sometimes. This is really something true, and there is where love comes—when it is demanding, and yet we can give it to Him with joy. Just as I have said today, I have said that if I don't go to Heaven for anything else I will be going to Heaven for all the publicity because it has purified me and sacrificed me and made me really ready to go to Heaven. I think that this is something, that we must live life beautifully, we have Jesus with us and He loves us. If we could only remember that God loves me, and I have an opportunity to love others as he loves me, not in big things, but in small things with great love, then Norway becomes a nest of love. And how beautiful it will be that from here a centre for peace has been given. That from here the joy of life of the unborn child comes out. If you become a burning light in the world of peace, then really the Nobel Peace Prize is a gift of the Norwegian people. God bless you!

INAUGURATION SPEECH

Nelson Mandela

In 1994, after years of struggle, and spending twenty-seven years in prison, Nelson Mandela became the first coloured man to be elected president of South

Africa. This is Mandela's famous speech, made at Cape Town on 10 May 1994, after being sworn in. Get your teeth into this piece by reading about the great man and understanding the years of hardship he suffered in order to realize his dream.

Your Majesties, Your Highnesses, Distinguished Guests, Comrades and Friends,

Today, all of us do, by our presence here, and by our celebrations in other parts of our country and the world, confer glory and hope to newborn liberty. Out of the experience of an extraordinary human disaster that lasted too long, must be born a society of which all humanity will be proud.

Our daily deeds as ordinary South Africans must produce an actual South African reality that will reinforce humanity's belief in justice, strengthen its confidence in the nobility of the human soul and sustain all our hopes for a glorious life for all. All this we owe both to ourselves and to the peoples of the world who are so well represented here today.

To my compatriots, I have no hesitation in saying that each one of us is as intimately attached to the soil of this beautiful country as are the famous jacaranda trees of Pretoria and the mimosa trees of the bushveld. Each time one of us touches the soil of this land, we feel a sense of personal renewal. The national mood changes as the seasons change. We are moved by a sense of joy and exhilaration when the grass turns green and the flowers bloom. That spiritual and physical oneness we all share with this common homeland explains the depth of the pain we all carried in our hearts as we saw our country tear itself apart in a terrible conflict, and as we saw it spurned, outlawed and isolated by the peoples of the world, precisely because it has become the universal base of the pernicious ideology and practice of racism and racial oppression.

We, the people of South Africa, feel fulfilled that humanity has taken us back into its bosom, that we, who were outlaws not so long ago, have today been given the rare privilege to be host to the nations of the world on our own soil. We thank all our distinguished international guests for having come to take possession with the people of our country of what is, after all, a common victory for justice, for peace, for human dignity. We trust that you will continue to stand by us as we tackle the challenges of building peace, prosperity, non-sexism, non-racialism and democracy.

We deeply appreciate the role that the masses of our people and their political mass democratic, religious, women, youth, business, traditional and other leaders have played to bring about this conclusion. Not least among them is my Second Deputy President, the Honourable F. W. de Klerk.

We would also like to pay tribute to our security forces, in all their ranks, for the distinguished role they have played in securing our first democratic elections and the transition to democracy, from bloodthirsty forces which still refuse to see the light.

The time for the healing of the wounds has come. The moment to bridge the chasms that divide us has come. The time to build is upon us.

We have, at last, achieved our political emancipation. We pledge ourselves to liberate all our people from the continuing bondage of poverty, deprivation, suffering, gender and other discrimination.

We succeeded to take our last steps to freedom in conditions of relative peace. We commit ourselves to the construction of a complete, just and lasting peace.

We have triumphed in the effort to implant hope in the breasts of the millions of our people. We enter into a covenant that we shall build the society in which all South Africans, both black and white, will be able to walk tall, without any fear in their hearts, assured of their inalienable right to human dignity—a rainbow nation at peace with itself and the world.

As a token of its commitment to the renewal of our country, the new Interim Government of National Unity will, as a matter of urgency, address the issue of amnesty for various categories of our people who are currently serving terms of imprisonment.

We dedicate this day to all the heroes and heroines in this country and the rest of the world who sacrificed in many ways and surrendered their lives so that we could be free.

Their dreams have become reality. Freedom is their reward.

We are both humbled and elevated by the honour and privilege that you, the people of South Africa, have bestowed on us, as the first president of a united, democratic, non-racial and non-sexist government.

We understand it still that there is no easy road to freedom.

We know it well that none of us acting alone can achieve success.

We must therefore act together as a united people, for national reconciliation, for nation building, for the birth of a new world.

Let there be justice for all. Let there be peace for all. Let there be work, bread, water and salt for all.

Let each know that for each the body, the mind and the soul have been freed to fulfil themselves.

Never, never and never again shall it be that this beautiful land will again experience the oppression of one by another and suffer the indignity of being the skunk of the world.

Let freedom reign. The sun shall never set on so glorious a human achievement!

God bless Africa!

EULOGY TO LADY DIANA

Charles Spencer

Lady Diana was beloved of the British public through the years she was married to Prince Charles, heir to the British throne. She died tragically in a car accident while being chased by over-zealous photographers in Paris. This is the touching eulogy by the ninth Earl Spencer to his sister Lady Diana, Princess of Wales, delivered on her funeral at Westminster Abbey, on 6 September 1997. It is an ideal piece for a young man in class IX-XII.

I stand before you today, the representative of a family in grief, in a country in mourning, before a world in shock.

We are all united, not only in our desire to pay our respects to Diana, but rather in our need to do so.

For such was her extraordinary appeal that the tens of millions of people taking part in this service all over the world, via television and radio, who never actually met her, feel that they, too, lost someone close to them in the early hours of Sunday morning. It is a more remarkable tribute to Diana than I can ever hope to offer her today.

Diana was the very essence of compassion, of duty, of style, of beauty. All over the world she was a symbol of selfless humanity, a standard-bearer for the rights of the truly downtrodden, a very British girl who transcended nationality. Someone with a natural nobility who was classless and who proved in the last year that she needed no royal title to continue to generate her particular brand of magic.

Today is our chance to say thank you for the way you brightened our lives, even though God granted you but half a life. We will all feel cheated always that you were taken from us so young, and yet we must learn to be grateful that you came along at all. Only now you are gone do we truly appreciate what we are now without, and we want you to know that life without you is very, very difficult.

We have all despaired at our loss over the past week, and only the strength of the message you gave us through your years of giving has afforded us the strength to move forward.

There is a temptation to rush to canonize your memory. There is no need to do so. You stand tall enough as a human being of unique qualities not to need to be seen as a saint.

Indeed, to sanctify your memory would be to miss out on the very core of your being, your wonderfully mischievous sense of humor, with a laugh that bent you double. Your joy for life transmitted wherever you took your smile and the sparkle in those unforgettable eyes. Your boundless energy, which you could barely contain.

But your greatest gift was your intuition, and it was a gift you used wisely. This is what underpinned all your other wonderful attributes, and if we look to analyse what it was about you that had such a wide appeal, we find it in your instinctive feel for what was really important in all our lives. Without your God-given sensitivity we would be immersed in greater ignorance at the anguish of AIDS and HIV sufferers, the plight of the homeless, the isolation of lepers, the random destruction of landmines.

Diana explained to me once that it was her innermost

feelings of suffering that made it possible for her to connect with her constituency of the rejected. And here we come to another truth about her. For all the status, the glamour, the applause, Diana remained throughout a very insecure person at heart, almost childlike in her desire to do good for others so she could release herself from deep feelings of unworthiness, of which her eating disorders were merely a symptom. The world sensed this part of her character and cherished her for her vulnerability whilst admiring her for her honesty.

The last time I saw Diana was on July 1, her birthday, in London, when typically she was not taking time to celebrate her special day with friends but was guest of honour at a fundraising charity evening. She sparkled of course, but I would rather cherish the days I spent with her in March when she came to visit me and my children in our home in South Africa. I am proud of the fact that, apart from when she was on public display meeting President Mandela, we managed to contrive to stop the ever-present paparazzi from getting a single picture of her—that meant a lot to her.

These were days I will always treasure. It was as if we had been transported back to our childhood when we spent such an enormous amount of time together—the two youngest in the family.

Fundamentally, she hadn't changed at all from the big sister who mothered me as a baby, fought with me at school and endured those long train journeys between our parents' homes with me at weekends.

It is a tribute to her level-headedness and strength that despite the most bizarre life imaginable after her childhood, she remained intact, true to herself.

There is no doubt that she was looking for a new direction

in her life at this time. She talked endlessly of getting away from England, mainly because of the treatment that she received at the hands of the newspapers. I don't think she ever understood why her genuinely good intentions were sneered at by the media, why there appeared to be a permanent quest on their behalf to bring her down. It is baffling.

My own and only explanation is that genuine goodness is threatening to those at the opposite end of the moral spectrum. It is a point to remember that of all the ironies about Diana, perhaps the greatest was this: a girl given the name of the ancient goddess of hunting was, in the end, the most hunted person of the modern age.

She would want us today to pledge ourselves to protecting her beloved boys William and Harry from a similar fate and I do this here, Diana, on your behalf. We will not allow them to suffer the anguish that used regularly to drive you to tearful despair.

And beyond that, on behalf of your mother and sisters, I pledge that we, your blood family, will do all we can to continue the imaginative and loving way in which you were steering these two exceptional young men, so that their souls are not simply immersed by duty and tradition, but can sing openly as you planned.

We fully respect the heritage into which they have both been born, and will always respect and encourage them in their royal role.

But we, like you, recognize the need for them to experience as many different aspects of life as possible to arm them spiritually and emotionally for the years ahead. I know you would have expected nothing less from us.

William and Harry, we all care desperately for you today.

We are all chewed up with sadness at the loss of a woman who was not even our mother. How great your suffering is we cannot even imagine.

I would like to end by thanking God for the small mercies he has shown us at this dreadful time, for taking Diana at her most beautiful and radiant and when she had joy in her private life.

Above all, we give thanks for the life of a woman I am so proud to be able to call my sister: the unique, the complex, the extraordinary and irreplaceable Diana, whose beauty, both internal and external, will never be extinguished from our minds.

TEACHER'S DAY SPEECH

A. P. J. Abdul Kalam

A. P. J. Abdul Kalam was without a doubt one of our country's most popular presidents. He had a unique rapport with the youth of the country. Here are excerpts from his address made over All India Radio on the eve of Teacher's Day on 4 September 2003. In this speech he talks about the three teachers, each completely different from the other, who influenced him at different critical stages of his life and helped mould him into what he is today.

Dear listeners of All India Radio and teachers, my greetings to all of you.

I am talking to you on the special occasion of Teacher's Day. On this day, we gratefully remember the great educationist Dr Sarvepalli Radhakrishnan, whose dream was that 'Teachers should be the best minds in the country'. Hence, Teacher's Day is very important for all our people, as the teachers lay the foundation for creating enlightened citizens for the nation. On this day, I would like to recall three teachers who helped me in shaping my life.

To begin with I am going to talk to you about my father Janab Avul Pakir Jainulabdeen, as a teacher. My father taught me a great lesson when I was a young boy. It was just after India got independence. My father was elected panchayat board member and on the same day he was also elected the president of the Rameswaram Panchayat Board. At that time they elected my father as panchayat board president not because he belonged to a particular religion or a particular caste or spoke a particular language or for his economic status. He was elected only on the basis of his nobility of mind and for being a good human being. Dear listeners, I would like to narrate one incident that took place on the day he was elected president of the panchayat board.

Those days we did not have electricity and we used to study under ration kerosene lamps. I was reading the lessons loudly and I heard a knock at the door. Somebody opened the door, came in and asked me where my father was? I told him that father had gone for the evening namaz. Then he said, I have brought something for him, can I keep it here? I asked the person to leave the item on the cot. After that I continued my studies.

I used to learn by reading aloud in my younger days. I was reading loud and fully concentrating on my studies. At that time my father came in and saw a tambalum kept in the cot. He opened the cover of the tambalum and found there was a costly dhoti, angawastram, some fruits and some sweets and he could see the slip that the person had left behind.

That was the first time I saw him very angry and also that

was the first time I had got a thorough beating from him. I got frightened and started weeping. My mother embraced and consoled me. Then my father came and touched my shoulder lovingly with affection and advised me not to receive any gift without his permission. Then he told me that it is not a good habit. A gift is always accompanied by some purpose and a gift is a dangerous thing. It is like touching a snake and getting the poison in turn. This lesson stands out always in my mind even when I am in my seventies.

When I think of my second teacher, I am reminded of my childhood days when I was studying in eighth class at the age of thirteen. I had a teacher, Shri Siva Subramania Iyer. All of us loved to attend his class. One day he was teaching about a bird's flight. He drew a diagram of a bird on the blackboard depicting the wings, tail and the body structure with the head. He explained how birds create the lift and fly. He also explained to us how they change direction while flying. At the end of the class, he wanted to know whether we understood how birds fly. I said, I did not understand. When I said this, the teacher asked the other students whether they understood or not. Many students said that they also did not understand. He did not get upset by our response since he was a committed teacher.

Our teacher said that he would take all of us to the seashore. That evening the whole class was at the seashore of Rameswaram. He showed the seabirds in formations of ten to twenty numbers. We saw the marvellous formations of birds with a purpose and we were all amazed. He showed us the birds and asked us to see that when the birds fly, what they looked like. We saw the wings flapping. He asked us to look at the tail portion with the combination of flapping wings and twisting tail. We noticed closely and found that the birds in that condition flew in the direction they desired. Then he asked us a question, 'Where is the engine and how is it powered?'

The bird is powered by its own life and the motivation of what it wants. All these things were explained to us within fifteen minutes. We all understood the dynamics from this practical example. Our teacher was a great teacher; he could give us a theoretical lesson coupled with a live practical example available in nature. This is real teaching. I am sure many of the teachers in schools and colleges will follow this example.

From that evening, I thought that my future study has to be with reference to flight and flight systems. I am saying this because my teacher's teaching and the event that I witnessed decided my future career. The bird flying exercise given by my teacher, really gave me a goal and a mission for my life. Thus my life was transformed as a rocket engineer, aerospace engineer and technologist. That one incident of my teacher teaching the lesson, showing the visual live example proved to be a turning point in my life which eventually shaped my profession.

A student during his school life up to 10+2 spends 25,000 hours in the school campus. His life is more influenced by the teachers and the school environment. Therefore, the school must have the best of teachers with ability to teach and love teaching. Teachers should become role models. Similarly, the student must be alert to build himself with the best of qualities and to get ignited with a vision for his future life.

I would like to share with you another experience with my teacher Prof. Satish Dhawan. First, I worked in Delhi with the Ministry of Defence. Later I joined the Defence Research and Development Organisation (DRDO) in 1958 at the Aeronautical Development Establishment at Bangalore. There, with the advice of the director, I took up the development of hovercraft. Hovercraft design needed the development of a ducted contra-rotating propeller for creating a smooth flow balancing the torques. I did not know how to design a contra-rotating propeller though I knew how to design a conventional propeller. Some of my friends told me that I could approach Prof. Satish Dhawan of the Indian Institute of Science, for help.

I took permission from my director and went to Prof. Dhawan who was sitting in a small room in the Indian Institute of Science with a lot of books in the background and a blackboard on the wall. I explained the problem. He told me that it was really a challenging task and he would teach me the design if I attended his classes from 2 p.m. to 3 p.m. on all Saturdays for the next six weeks.

He was a visionary teacher. He prepared the schedule for the entire course and wrote it on the blackboard. He also gave me the reference material and books I should read before I start attending the course. Before commencing each meeting, he would ask critical questions and assess my understanding of the subject. That was for the first time that I realized how a good teacher prepares himself for teaching with meticulous planning and prepares the student for acquisition of knowledge. This process continued for the next six weeks. I got the capability for designing the contra-rotating propeller. That was the time I realized that Prof. Dhawan was not only a teacher but also a fantastic development engineer of aeronautical systems.

Later during the critical phases of testing, Prof. Dhawan was with me to witness the test and find solutions to the problems. After reaching the smooth test phase, the contra-rotating propeller went through fifty hours of continuous testing. Prof. Dhawan witnessed the test himself and congratulated me. However, at that time, I did not realize that Prof. Dhawan would become chairman, ISRO, and that I would get the opportunity to work with him as a project director in the development of the satellite launch vehicle SLV-3 for injecting the Rohini satellite into the orbit. Nature has its own way to link the student's dream and real life later.

This was the first design in my career which gave me the confidence to design many complex aerospace systems in future. Through this project I learnt the techniques of designing and developing the contra-rotating propeller. Above all, I learnt that in a project, problems will always crop up; we should not allow problems to be our masters but we should defeat the problems.

The three teachers in my life; what did they give me? Any enlightened human being can be created by three unique characteristics. One is moral value system. That I got from my father the hard way. Secondly, the teacher becoming a role model. Not only does the student learn, but the teacher shapes his life with great dreams and aims. Finally, the education and learning process has to culminate in the creation of professional capability leading to confidence and will power to make a design, to make a product, to make a system, bravely combating many problems. What a fortune and blessing I had from my three teachers.

Among the listeners, there may be many parents, many teachers and a large number of students. Every one of us in this planet creates a page in human history irrespective of who he or she is. I realize my experience is a small dot in human life, but that dot has a life and light. This light, let it light many lamps.

My best wishes to all of you on this occasion of Teacher's Day. Thank you.

ACKNOWLEDGEMENTS

I would like to thank Andrew Scolt and Shane Alieu for their help in compiling the pieces; and Ronald Gass for being the only elocution coach I ever had.

My publishers and I would also like to acknowledge the following for permission to reproduce copyright material:

Sourcebooks, Inc., for the poem 'The Tiger and the Zebra' from Kenn Nesbitt's *My Hippo Has the Hiccups: And Other Poems I Totally Made Up*;

Keki N. Daruwalla for the poem 'Tiger', which was first published by Ratna Sagar P. Ltd.;

Oxford University Press India, New Delhi, for the poem 'Night of the Scorpion' from *Collected Poems: Nissim Ezekiel*;

Roald Dahl and Penguin Books UK for the poem 'Television' from *Charlie and the Chocolate Factory*;

The Estate of Kamala Das for the extract from the poem 'An Introduction';

The Estate of Robert William Service for the poem 'The Cremation of Sam McGee';

Penguin Books India for the poem 'The Hare and the Tortoise' from Vikram Seth's *Beastly Tales from Here and There*;

'Why Can't the English' words by Alan Jay Lerner, music by Frederick Loewe © 1956 (renewed) Chappell & Co., Inc. (ASCAP)

'I'm an Ordinary Man' words by Alan Jay Lerner, music by Frederick Loewe © 1956 (renewed) Chappell & Co., Inc. (ASCAP)

Penguin Books India for the story 'The Kitemaker' from Ruskin Bond's *The Best of Ruskin Bond: Delhi Is Not Far*;

The Estate of Dennis Potter for the extract 'The Son of Man' from the eponymous television play.

Bhuvaneshwari Srinivasamurthy of Indian Thought Publications for the story 'Trail of the Green Blazer' by R. K. Narayan;

Oxford University Press India, New Delhi, for the speeches 'A Tryst With Destiny' and 'The Light Has Gone Out of Our Lives' from *Nehru's India: Select Speeches*, edited by Mushirul Hasan;

Extract from 'Nobel Prize Lecture' by Mother Teresa © The Nobel Foundation 1979;

The Nelson Mandela Centre of Memory for 'Inauguration Speech' by Nelson Mandela;

The Estate of Earl and Countess Spencer for the speech 'Eulogy to Lady Diana';

Dr A. P. J. Abdul Kalam for his 'Teacher's Day Speech'.